Along the Way Home

Along the Way Home

JERRY W. MIXON

BROADMAN PRESS
Nashville, Tennessee

Copyright © 1989 • Broadman Press
All rights reserved
4250-64
ISBN: 0-8054-5064-5

Dewey Decimal Classification: 248.4
Subject Heading: CHRISTIAN LIFE // COUNTRY LIFE
Library of Congress Catalog Card Number: 88-22974

Printed in the United States of America

Unless otherwise indicated, all Scripture quotations are from the King James Version of the Bible. Quotations marked (NASB) are from the *New American Standard Bible*. Copyright © The Lockman Foundation, 1960, 1962, 1963, 1968, 1971, 1972, 1973, 1975, 1977. Used by permission.

Library of Congress Cataloging-in-Publication Data

Mixon, Jerry W., 1940-
  Along the way home / Jerry W. Mixon.
    p. cm.
  ISBN 0-8054-5064-5
  1. Meditations. 2. Country life—Southern States. 3. Mixon, Jerry W., 1940-   . 4. Southern States—Social life and customs—1865-   I. Title.
BV4832.2.M537   1989
242—dc19   88-22974

Foreword

Jerry Mixon knows what all good communicators know. Of course our Lord Christ knew it. All the great preachers have known it. People think in pictures—not in logical, orderly sequence—but pictures.

This book is a delightful collection of word pictures laid alongside the vital truths of God's Word. Like our Lord, the author verbally shows us what he means. It is good and helpful reading.

It is good to have another tour of the large and small lessons found "off the main road."

FRANK POLLARD, *Pastor*
First Baptist Church
Jackson, Mississippi

Contents

The Wonder of It All	13
Riding a Stick Horse	16
Country Manners	18
Starving to Death	21
Snipe Hunting	24
Behind the Stove	27
Hand-Me-Downs	30
Buried Treasure	33
Mad Dog	37
Family Ties	40
Charlie's Song	43
Bricks from the Brickyard	46
Harvesttime	48
The Singing Log	51
Fires of Coal	54
Mississippi Mud House	57
Can You Take a Dare?	60
The Way Home	63
Squirrel Hunting	66
On the Road Again	69
Cat in the Box	72
Someone in the Stands	75

Does God Play Fair?	78
Creed or Confidence	81
God Loves Jesus	84
What Is Above God's Name?	86
My Mad Mirror	88
The White Suit	91
Don't Rain on My Parade	94
Trivial Pursuit	97
Hurry Up and Wait	100
My Friend Downey	103
Fun Being His	106
Mule Eggs for Sale	109
Staying on Track	112
You Can Go Home Again	115
Look for Me When You See Me Coming	118
Keepers of the Well	121
Home Before Dark	124

Introduction

Dark was the path that led from our house to Uncle Carl's. It made no difference whether you walked it during the daylight hours or in the still of night; it was always a path of darkness. Many years of growth had allowed the trees on either side to grow tall and strong. They had also grown in such a fashion that they hung over the path and crowded out the noonday sun. Only a splash of sunlight here and there was allowed into this maze of bush and bramble.

Many were the days I made that trip up to Uncle Carl's house to borrow a cup of sugar or a pan of flour. If memory serves me correctly, it was only about three hundred yards through the woods. The trail or path, as we called it, was nothing more than a beaten-down walkway. Years before it had been a road of sorts but too many summers had come and gone for it to be anything more now than a trail. Nevertheless, I can remember as if it were yesterday.

Everytime I left the house my mother gave me two instructions. First, if I were to be gone for a long period of time, she would say, "You be sure to be home before dark." Secondly, if it was a trip of urgent need, like going after a cup of sugar, she would say, "Don't stop and play on your way home."

Now Mother knew the inside and outside of a boy like most folks know the alphabet. She knew that one frog or one doodlebug that dared to stick his head above ground was sure to catch my attention. Thus she warned me not to get sidetracked. Now included in the warning was a note to be sure and tell her everything that happened to me on my journey. No sooner would I return home than she would say something to the tune of, "Everything go all right?" or "Did you have any trouble along the way?" You see, my mother was so concerned that she had to know every detail. When I did share with her that I was tempted to sit a spell under a shade tree and watch a bird build her nest or try to catch one frog, she would always take time to explain the dangers of my temptations. There were times when I would see something in the woods or have a fear because of the dark wooded area and she would, in her own way, explain my reason for fear.

Many years have come and gone since those walks down that path, and sometimes I long for the simplicity of the wants, hurts, and fears of those days. The path I walk today and, for that matter, the path we all walk has many pitfalls. The trail is filled with more temptations and obstructions much more thorny than bush and brambles. There are no more temptations to chase a rabbit or catch a frog. My temptations now are to do less than my best or to take credit when credit is not due.

These are the days of manhood, not childhood. Yet there is that voice within that keeps saying, "Don't stop and play on your way home." I am not going after a cup of sugar now, or a pan of flour, but "I press toward the mark for the prize of the high calling of God in Christ Jesus" (Phil. 3:14). There is a greater goal to be achieved. I see many more troubles, trials, temptations, and times of testing; but, thank God, I know that at the close of day, when I have made that final step, my Heavenly Father will greet me as Mother did. No longer will I receive a pat on the head for a job well done, but a "crown of righteousness" (2 Tim. 4:8). Then, with words of comfort and wisdom, my Father will take me in His arms and explain my journey and all that happened to me ALONG THE WAY HOME (1 Cor. 13:9-12).

The Wonder of It All

Ephesians 3:20　　*"Now unto him that is able to do exceeding abundantly above all that we ask or think."*

The other day while looking through some old pictures I came across a picture of me sitting by the old pump in the backyard of our Lakeview home. We had running water. We just had to run outside to get it. Dressed in a striped shirt and overalls that came about two inches short of my brown high-top shoes, I was sitting on a board held up by two old rusty barrels. In the background you can see a day's washing hanging on the clothesline. I remember sometimes in the night the white clothes would appear as ghosts dancing in our yard. The evening breeze gave them movement and the loose-hanging clothesline made them bounce up and down.

A cardboard box is in my hand. I suppose this was my old treasure chest. You probably had one, too. Remember, this is where you kept all of your special items. Why, in this box I had special bottle caps that, if you lifted the cork out of them, would stick on your shirt like a badge. There was my special pocketknife, not very sharp, but it had a can opener and a screwdriver. The box also contained items like special baseball cards and candy wrappers saved from our Saturday trips to town.

Childhood has a way of creating interests that usually do not last for a lifetime. Most of the things we are interested in then are usually of no great value. At least most of those things were not very expensive. Then as we grow older our interests change. We begin to hold more important values, and the price tag of our interests will increase.

Yet somewhere along the way I wish I could keep that childlike wonder. You know the excitement of the "unexpected," like when you entered a room filled with strangers, all the time wondering which one was the evil enemy lurking behind his human mask. Oh, and remember the thrill of walking through a large department store for the first time. Why, you could see so much and you wished Mom would slow down so you could take it all in. The wonder of childhood at Christmas. Somehow I wish all of us could hold that magic wonder of childhood in our Christian life. You know the excitement when you do something "for the first time."

Just think how much more exciting our worship services would be if we entered with that kind of attitude. You know, the attitude that something is going to happen and not the attitude that we are afraid something will happen. If we could just capture some of the wonder and magic of childhood, we might be like the man Jesus spoke of who was plowing in the field and discovered a treasure. *Have we lost the surprise of the kingdom?* Has anything in our Christian experience become so routine and mundane that we just don't expect God to break through and do the unexpected? Is it really true that most of us do not believe God can do any more than we can do? Have we confined Him to a limited place and time? Do we in reality say each week, "God, you have one hour in which to act. If you do not do something before twelve o'clock, we are going home."

Oh, the cry of my soul is that I will not lose the surprise of the kingdom. I will be like the merchant man seeking goodly pearls, but always leaving room for finding the pearl of great price (Matt. 13:45-46). Daily I pray that I will not try to reason God out into some logical pattern of speaking, acting, or teaching me. Daily I will look for that surprise of the kingdom. My prayer is that God will help me keep alive that wonderful excitement of the unexpected in my Christian faith.

At the bottom of the photo from my childhood days, I can see a shadow. That shadow is cast by my father. Dad was taking the picture. I need to remember my life is not lived alone, for my Heavenly Father is always near to give me the surprise of His kingdom. Have you figured God out? Do you know just how He will operate in your life today? Do you already have your day and life all planned out? What I am asking is, do you leave room for the will of God in your life to change? All of us should enter each day with the thought and openness that God can do something today in my life that I have not planned or even thought of. *Today* could be a delightful surprise.

Riding a Stick Horse

1 John 1:9   *"If we confess . . . he is faithful and just to forgive us."*

Dust rose from my bare feet as I dug my hands into my side. I dashed my stick horse through the bushes and raced down the lane. Just ahead I imagined Black Bart and his band of train robbers counting their loot. I slowed to a trot, then a walk. Leaning my stick horse against a tree limb, I reached for my trusty Red Rider pistols. As I pulled my hands up from the holsters, I realized my guns had fallen out. In complete confusion, I dropped to my knees and tears burst like rain falling on a tin roof. What was I to do? My older brother, Robert, had just brought these two guns home from Germany. He had been in the army and I had taken such pride in them. How was I to face Robert and Mother? Uh, oh, the thought of Mom caused me to leap on my stick horse and race back down through the sagebrush field and across the creek, keeping a searching eye for my two trusty guns, as well as for Black Bart and his gang.

Memory fails me now about what happened that day when I returned home with two empty holsters. It does say something to me and that is, it must not have been too much of a traumatic experience. By that I mean they must have all forgiven me. I do believe, in recollection, had Mom made a trip to the peach tree or if Robert had been too upset, I am sure I would have remembered. The fact that the rest of that day lies secretly in my memory, at least to me, means that a tired, broken little boy came home to waiting arms of forgiveness. Arms that caressed and soothed his hurt, arms that poured warm water in an old tub and made sure that a country boy washed behind his ears, arms that pulled a tattered older brother's shirt about his shivering body and sent him off to bed with a pat on the head and a good-night kiss.

You know, the longer I live the more I am convinced that God is kind and tender in His dealing with us. Daily, we, through our carelessness or neglect, lose that precious resource God has given us called time. We abuse and misuse many wonderful hours that flee ever so fast. Then at the close of the day we face the reality of moments gone. Now we shudder to face our Redeemer in prayer, but there in that quiet moment we find again those waiting arms of forgiveness. Perhaps the words of an unknown poet say it best:

> I went to the Throne with a quivering soul—
>   The old year was done.
> "Dear Father, hast Thou a new leaf for me?
>   I have spoiled this one.
> He took the old leaf, stained and blotted,
>   And gave me a new one, all unspotted,
>   And into my sad heart smiled:
>   "Do better now, my child!"

Country Manners

Micah 7:1   *"My soul desired the firstripe fruit."*

When supper was over at our house, we would always find one piece of meat left on the table. If we had pie for dessert, we would see one lonely piece left on the plate. The reason was very simple. Dad said we were to always leave one piece for manners. Well, one night I slipped back into the kitchen after everyone had gone to bed and that was when I found out who manners was. Dad was sitting there eating the last piece of pie. Of course, we all understood his reasoning. Dad believed in manners and all the other stuff that went along with them. For instance, we always said, "Yes, ma'am" and "No, ma'am." We were taught this from birth.

Have you ever thought how rude we are to God? How often do we say a prayer of thanksgiving for all the good things that come our way? Very often we rush into His presence with some little give-me prayer. I promise this, we would not rush up to my Dad with a request. He taught us to walk into his presence and to address him properly. Seems to me that Jesus had something to say about our addressing and entering our Father's presence. Do I remember His words correctly? When you pray say, "Our Father which art in heaven" (Matt. 6:9; Luke 11:2). Why, way back in the Old Testament we are told to "Be still, and know that I am God" (Ps. 46:10). Goodness, our manners with God are very important. As a matter of fact, I think one of the major sins of the church today is ingratitude. Many of us sit around the table of plenty, but we are not grateful to our God who has supplied the bounty. God, help us to learn to mind our manners.

Now, Mother was not left out of the manners department either. I well remember that she taught us when we had company to let them sit in the best chair. We were instructed to open the door for girls and, above anything, never hit a girl. A fellow was embarrassed the other night after church when he opened the door for his wife. She looked at him rather amazed and said, "Are you getting in on my side? Am I driving?" I knew in a minute his manners were for show. It was obvious he had not opened the door for her in a long, long time, if ever before. If we are to exercise manners with our family and friends, how much more should we be on our toes with God?

Let me ask you some questions and you check out your manners. The last time you prayed, did you meditate on God before you rushed into His presence? Have you ever prayed just a prayer of thanksgiving to God? This would be a great time now to begin to check your manners with God.

Oh, yes, I almost forgot, but Mom used to make us always let our guest have first choice of the food on the plate. That is a great spiritual lesson. The Bible declares God as saying, "My soul desired the firstripe fruit" (Mic.

7:1). God is in our life by invitation. We have invited Him in. He is a King who rules only by invitation. If He is our guest, and He is, does it not seem right to give Him first choice in all we do?

Starving to Death

Matthew 5:6   *"Blessed are they which do hunger."*

When Mr. Lott finally stopped the bus in front of our house we ran over the railroad tracks and across the yard like a jackrabbit running during the Depression. Once inside the house we looked for a biscuit that we could punch a hole in with our finger. I remember my sister made some once we could not kick a hole in. Anyway, after we made the hole, we usually filled it with jam or syrup. Sometimes we walked into the backyard and picked some blackberries. After placing them in a bowl, we poured milk and sugar over them for a great snack. Our favorite words when entering the house were, "I'm starving." Guess what my children say today when they come home from school. You guessed it—the same thing. Now we were not starving, nor are they; but this ritual became a habit. Most of us have the habit that when we bend our elbow, our mouth flies open.

I can remember, after eating like that, when Mom had supper ready we would gather at the table. Most of the time we would not be hungry. Mom would say, "Eat your supper before it gets cold." We would always respond, "I am not hungry." Then she would say very firmly, "Eat!" Now Mother could make us eat, but she could never make us hungry. You see, hunger is something that is natural.

Do you remember when Jesus was teaching on the mountainside, He said, "Blessed are they which do hunger and thirst after righteousness: for they shall be filled" (Matt. 3:5)? I believe He was giving us the conclusion of the work of the Holy Spirit in preparation for a person being saved. In verse 3 He had said, "Blessed are the poor," and this was a reference to spiritual poverty. Blessed or godly happiness belongs to those who realize they are spiritually broken. They are dependent on some outside power just like anyone who is financially poor.

Then He said, "Blessed are they that mourn" (v. 4). This was not a note to remind us that all those who go around weeping will be happy. I knew a lady once who always felt bad, but one day she got mixed up and said, "I feel good." However, it did not take her long to discover her mistake and quickly she added, "But you know, Preacher, every time I feel good I get to feeling bad—because I know how bad I will feel when I am not feeling good." Jesus was not speaking of folks like that. He was talking of a progression.

Godly happiness belongs to those who mourn over the discovery they have made. They mourn over their spiritual poverty. Then He said, in effect, "If they do not let pride get in the way. If they will stay meek, something will happen in their life." God will step in, and when God steps in, He will create a natural hunger and thirst for righteousness. I think sometimes we have tried to create that in folks. We have not trusted the Word of God to be that quick and powerful two-edged sword. So often we have tried to grow the seed and were not willing to sow and wait for the harvest. Little wonder we have thousands of church members that we cannot find. Little wonder 20 percent of our church members give 80 percent of the church budget. Little wonder we have a faithful few who serve and support the church.

Let us not just try to bring people unto conviction; let us present the Word that presents the Man. When we have planted the seed, some will grow. Yes, some will be choked by the cares of this world. The devil will steal the truth from the hearts of some, and some seed will fall by the wayside on unreceptive hearts, but praise God, some will fall on good ground. When the Word hits the good ground (those who hear and are open) it will create a natural desire for God, and God will fill their souls.

There is yet another note. If we do not have a natural desire for godliness, something is wrong. Do you have to be pushed, prodded, and paddled into Christian service or to seek right living? If you do, my friend, something in your life is unnatural. You see, the absence of food causes hunger; and the recognition of His absence followed by sorrow and humility has set the stage for God to sweep into our lives and fill us.

Snipe Hunting

John 8:44 "*He was a murderer from the beginning. . . . There is no truth in him.*"

Folks, if you have never been snipe hunting then you have never been hunting. Now some people do not believe snipe even exist, but they do. They are wading birds belonging to the Gallinago Macrorhamphus, thus you can usually find them in low, wet marshy places. They have a long bill that is used to dig worms and they have long slender legs with no feathers on them. The legs that is. In the United States the most common snipe is the Gallinago Wilson's snipe, sometimes called jacksnipe.

Memory fails me if I have to give you an age when I first heard about snipe but, boy, I will never forget what a time it was. You see, I had these two older brothers who were very interested in my education. They made sure I did not miss anything growing up, and this night would be no different. Robert and Joe made sure that I understood it was my job to hold the sack open. They made sure that I understood it was up to me whether we caught any snipe. The instructions were that I was not to move, no matter what. "Don't worry about anything," they said, "just make sure you keep the sack low on the ground and wait.

We will go out in the woods and drive them out. When you hear them running, hold the sack open and *bingo* we got us a mess of snipe." These were my instructions and so there I stood. There is no way I can tell you how many cold chills ran up and down my spine. It is just beyond me how many times I felt the cold hand of fear brush against the side of my face. Once I knew I felt the hot breath of a bear, lion, or something on the back of my neck. I was too scared to look. There I stood, frozen to the spot, half bent over, holding a croker sack wide open waiting for snipe to run out of the woods. Tall trees angrily pointed their fingers to the sky while others rushed out of the moonlit night like would-be ghosts.

So often in life I find my brothers and sisters in that same type of spiritual arena. They are confused and alone in life. There is a sense of loneliness. Everything appears out of focus and out of shape. Nothing seems real. At the same time, everything that is real appears false. There they are, standing in the middle of life with their little sack. They have spent the better part of life trying to catch the would-be snipe—only to find at the conclusion of the night the joke's on them.

I can still remember after standing in that position and in that state of fear for several hours, I finally threw the sack down and ran home. Upon my arrival I found my two brothers sound asleep in bed.

Jesus said it this way: "What shall it profit a man, if he shall gain the whole world, and lose his own soul?" (Mark 8:36). So many folks living in this world have tied themselves down to things. You see, that is why we have so hard of a time giving our money to God. Money is material blessing and, for the most part, we are just too tied to things.

You know, the fact is, no man has ever "[gained] the

whole world." No man ever will. Just think of that. Jesus did not say we could profit if we sold our soul for folly. He did not say we could profit if we sold our soul for power or prestige. What Jesus did say was what no man can ever do and that was gain the whole world. Yes, Jesus said if you could gain it all—not just part of it, not just the Rockefeller fortune, *but if you could gain it all*—you would fall short of what your soul (life) is worth.

Almost a century ago a boat loaded with miners returning from the goldfields of California was slowly making its way up the Mississippi River. When the boat struck something in the river it began to sink. There were not enough lifeboats and many of the miners unfastened their belts heavy with gold and let them fall on the deck of the sinking ship. Free from the weight of the gold, they swam ashore. One miner gathered up some of the belts and fastened them around his body. When he leaped into the water he sank as if he had been made of lead. Several days later when they found his body, no one congratulated him upon his vast amount of wealth.

The great thing about snipe hunting is that you only go once. After that no one can fool you again. Would it not be great if we could all learn the lesson of profit and loss once and never be fooled again?

Behind the Stove

Psalm 34:9　　　*"There is no want to them that fear him."*

We all gathered around the kitchen stove. Just outside our back door, no more than ten feet away, lay the railroad tracks. I could see the iron rails shining in the afternoon sun. Just about twenty-five yards on the other side of the tracks Bouie River wound its way toward the south. Straight in front of our house was the Lakeview road. We had moved further out in the country. But now we had grass instead of dirt in our front yard. Needless to say, with the road, the tracks, and the river all within reach we hardly ever had a dull moment at our house. If Mom was not shouting, "You kids, get out of the road," she was yelling, "and don't you dare go near that river."

Standing closer to the stove I waited for some additional news about Dad. My father, Earl Mixon, no longer worked for Dunn's Grocery. He had long since become a truck driver for West Brothers. Because of this increase in pay we had moved further out but now we had indoor plumbing. It was close to Christmas and Dad had a regular route to Jackson, Mississippi. A freak ice and snowstorm had him snowbound in our capital city and we all wondered if we would have any Christmas at all.

Robert, Joe, Sue, Pat, and I hovered near the stove, waiting for Mom to share some good news for a change. Finally she spoke, "Your Dad will be here tomorrow." Word had come that the road would be open the following day and we all shouted for joy.

Memory does not serve me well about how the night ended, but I am sure that we all went to bed feeling rather relieved. At least for now the hope of trucks and toys was back in our minds again. I do remember what happened the following day.

Dad arrived late in the afternoon and we had prepared a fire in the kitchen. I remember standing behind the old wood stove and watching Dad as he sat eating at the table. My Dad liked quiet when he ate and we obeyed his command. Well, Mom was standing near the stove warming something else for Dad when I reached over and pulled on her apron. With a gentle tug, I looked into her eyes and said, "Everything is going to be all right; Dad is home now." She smiled back and I rested further back in the corner behind the stove, convinced of my security.

Albert Einstein said, "I never think of the future. It comes soon enough." So many of us spend most of our life worrying about something. All the water in the world can never sink a ship if it never gets inside. Worry can sink our lives. It can make us miserable. Most of my childhood was not spent in worry. The solution for me at a very early age was my father. My whole world was wrapped up in him. His presence to me signified all was well. I put my trust in him.

Oh, how I wish I might carry that same attitude into my adult Christian experience. So many times I worry about life, knowing well that God is still in control of my life. Let us all remember Dad is home—God is on His throne and He never slumbers or sleeps. Because of this we can feel secure.

An elderly lady was asked the secret of her long life. She leaned back and said, "When I work, I work hard; when I sits, I sits easy; and when I worry, I go to sleep." No need to worry—Dad is home.

Hand-Me-Downs

Hebrews 2:1 *"Therefore we ought to give the more earnest heed to the things which we have heard, lest at any time we should let them slip."*

Early in my childhood I learned that if you were going to keep your chewing gum for a long time you had to make sure it was kept in a safe place. Chewing gum in the early forties was not easy to come by and even harder to hang on to. If you laid it down where your brother or sister could get their hands on it, you could kiss it good-bye. They never thought a second time about it being ABC gum. You know, already been chewed. We learned not to stick it on or under our plate at the table. If we happened to forget about it and left the table, then we never saw it again. The best place to keep gum was behind your ear. Should you forget about it you did not have to worry because someone was sure to ask, "What is that behind your ear?" Now, we also learned you could stick it on the bedpost overnight. The next morning it might be a little hard but after a few minutes in your mouth it was as good as new. Sometimes it would pull some of the paint off the bedpost and this gave a new flavor to the otherwise thoroughly chewed mass in your mouth. If we did not have gum, we would chew tar from a blacktop road or sweet gum from a tree near our house.

Our family not only learned to conserve gum, but we also learned to pass down clothes. We wore hand-me-downs. It was really something to have a brand-new, store-bought shirt. I think I was about twelve before I had my first shirt bought from Sears. All of the other times I had to wear shirts handed down from my two older brothers, Robert and Joe, or from my cousin, John Harris. It really was not that bad and I am happy that Mom did not make me wear my older sisters' hand-me-downs.

Now shoes were a different matter. I hated to wear other peoples' shoes. When I finally got a pair from my older brothers, they had worn them so long that you could step on a dime and I could tell you if it was heads or tails. The shoestrings were also a problem. They had been broken and tied together so many times that you could not tie them tight because the knots would not slip through the eyelets.

There were, of course, other things we passed down also. We passed down knowledge. We gave each other secrets like just how far you could push Dad before he would give you a licking. How to make a frog appear on your arm and how to cross your eyes are just some of the important matters passed on to me from my older brothers. They taught me how to pretend and opened up a whole new world for me through imagination. Thus, from clothes, shoes, secrets, and special instructions, we learned how to live with each other.

In the New Testament we have an earnest plea given to us by the author of Hebrews when he says, "We ought to give the more earnest heed to the things which we have heard, lest at any time we should let them slip" (2:1). The *New American Standard* Bible uses the word *drift* and it may be translated "to be carried past." The idea is not that they were drifting but that something was drifting past them. What a lesson for us today! If we are to win the world, we must not allow the world to drift past us. We must take that which has been handed down to us, namely, the gospel, and teach it to others. We must cling tenaciously to the hand-me-downs and pass them on. Indeed, we are to do what Paul later advised young Timothy to do, "And the things that thou has heard of me . . . the same commit thou to faithful men, who shall be able to teach others also" (2 Tim. 2:2).

Buried Treasure

Matthew 13:44 *"The kingdom of heaven is like unto a treasure hidden in the field; which a man found, and hid; and in his joy he goeth and selleth all that he hath, and buyeth that field" (ASV).*

Sometimes summer afternoons in Lakeview were rather lazy. If we were not sitting in the old beechnut tree down by the creek, we were usually swimming. One hot summer day, Jerry and Bud Sumeral showed up with a map. It was supposed to be the detailed plan on how to find a buried treasure. Needless to say, the afternoon was spent seeking but never finding. It did, however, give us a feeling of excitement. As we ran through the woods we had visions of pirate ships plowing through the sea. We could see in our mind's eye diamonds and gold pieces waiting in some secluded treasure chest. We never found the yellow brick road and that pot of gold that is supposed to be at the end of every rainbow. You can forget it too, because all we ever found was nothing. Yet, as I look back, the map and each rainbow gave us a new zeal for life. A rather dull summer day turned into an afternoon of thrills all because of two little words, *buried treasure.*

Jesus told a story once of a man plowing in a field. His days had been spent like most of those lazy summer days of ours. He did not own this field. He was only a sharecropper. He worked the field and received some of the benefits, but the joy of working for himself was not his. His days were all pretty much the same. He rose early in the morning and worked till almost dark. He went to bed and rose again the next day to the same routine. What Jesus did not say is that years before, a wealthy man had probably lived nearby but word had come of an invading army. Since there were no banks to protect his wealth, this man went out into the dark of night and buried his treasure in the field. When the army arrived he was taken prisoner, carried out of the country, and later died in prison. The secret of his treasure died with him.

Someone else now owns this field and the farmer is working it again today. His treadmill existence is about to change. Something is going to happen today that will change his life. Suddenly his plow scrapes an object beneath the soil. The farmer slowly walks back and begins to brush the dirt aside, intending to remove another of those large stones that lay just beneath the topsoil. The sunlight causes a bright flash to dart from the soil. The farmer brushes dirt faster for he, too, has heard tales of treasure buried deep in the earth. With the dirt removed and partially opened by the plow, he discovers a small chest filled with precious jewels and small gold coins. Quickly, Jesus adds this note to the story: "The kingdom of heaven is like unto treasure hid in a field; the which when a man hath found, he hideth, and for joy thereof goeth and selleth all that he hath, and buyeth that field" (Matt. 13:44). So the farmer secured the treasure for himself.

When you think of your Christian faith, how many folks do you know who treat it as a treasure? Most people consider it more of a burden than a blessing. Our attitude betrays us, for we just do not consider our faith to be a treasure. Our lack of faith in an effort to attain the treasure is evidence enough that we simply do not consider it of much value. Oh, in times of emergency, yes, it is of great value, but on a daily basis we could rate it about a two on a scale of one to ten.

Our lack of effort to maintain the kingdom is evidence that we do not consider it of much worth. We would rather amass the wealth of this world. If the kingdom means Bible study, worship, and ministry to others, we may do it, but only after we have done other things. You see, our carelessness with the treasure shows our lack of respect for it. Frankly, many Christians simply do not have time for God.

The diamond mines of Africa were discovered when a man rode by some boys playing marbles with some rough, crude objects. They were, in fact, rolling rough diamonds. The fact that the rough stones were treated as common glass did not rob them of their value, but it kept the boys from taking advantage of all they possessed. So many of God's people today are like that. They possess a treasure. Their faith is priceless. Their attitude toward it does not rob it of its value, but the way they treat their faith often keeps them from taking advantage of all they possess.

In McGuffey's story of a man of great wealth he told of the old miser who would sit for hours in the cellar of his home. There he would allow the gold coins to slip through his fingers saying, "My beauties ... my beauties." One day the wind blew the trapdoor closed and there was no one to hear his cry. Years later his skeleton was found along with his treasure. A rich skeleton, we might add, but his treasure could not give him life. His treasure took his life.

The faith of every believer gives him not only life in the eternal heavens but it gives him hope and zest and thrills in this life. It is the only treasure worth possessing, for it satisfies the deepest longings of the heart. It is the only treasure worth possessing, for when you have this treasure you have it all. Jesus said, "Seek ye first the kingdom of God . . . and all these things shall be added unto you" (Matt. 6:33). Let us take a fresh look at our attitude toward our faith today, in the hope that we will discover we really do have a buried treasure.

Mad Dog

1 Samuel 2:9 *"He will keep the feet of his saints."*

Word spread fast in our little community. It did not make any difference what kind of word it was; when those who were well off enough to have a phone had a word, they shared it. Anyway, most of the houses in Lakeview were close enough that a good country shout would carry from house to house. It was a hot summer day when I first heard the words, *mad dog*. I can remember the cold shiver it sent up and down my spine. We all knew what a mad dog was and we knew it was something to be feared. Mom quickly gathered all of the children into the house and locked the wooden front door. Peering out through the front window I had a clear view of the dog as he came down the road. He did not come toward our house, but he walked in sort of a right and then left pattern.

When he came to Mr. Homer Huggins's mailbox he turned into the yard and made his way straight up the big high steps that led to their front porch. We were all terrified, thinking the dog would try to get through the door. He never stopped but made his way from one end of the porch to the other, all the while foam dripping from his mouth. The very thought of being bitten by something like that made me hurt in the chest. After his visit to the porch, the mad dog left and continued down the road. Someone found one of the men in the community and after the dog disappeared around the curve near Mixon graveyard, we heard a rifle shot and that was the end of that.

I can still remember going over to Mr. Huggins's house to see if Mrs. Clara was all right. Mom gave us strict orders to be sure and not step in the foam from the dog's mouth. We were, of course, barefooted, and she was afraid the foam would enter our bloodstream through a cut or break in the skin. I was very careful where I walked and made sure that my feet stayed clear of any mad-dog foam. It was difficult to sleep that night, for images of the dog wandering down the road weighed heavily on my mind.

If there is one cry heard from my youth that I listen for daily it is the instruction "watch your step." So many in our day have fallen by the wayside because they did not watch where they were going. It is so easy to be lured off the narrow way. The way of the world is broad and tempting. There are so many tempting shortcuts that we sometimes lose sight of where we place our feet to take a stand. The writer of Proverbs talks about those whose feet are swift to shed blood and run to evil. As we travel through this world Paul tells us some things to avoid as he wrote to the church of Ephesus. In chapter 4 he said, "Put away lying, speak the truth with your neighbors," and he continues, "when you get angry, do not sin. Give no place for the devil and do not steal, but rather work for that you have and be generous to give to those in need" (vv. 25-28, author's paraphrase).

He calls for us to be kind to one another, tenderhearted, and forgiving. He is simply crying out, "Watch your step."

The writer of Hebrews says, "Make straight paths for your feet" (Heb. 12:13). Proverbs reminds us, "Ponder the path of thy feet, and let all thy ways be established. Turn not to the right hand nor to the left: remove thy foot from evil" (Prov. 4:26-27).

Let us all remember the faithful words recorded in 1 Samuel 2:9 where the writer reminds us, "He will keep the feet of his saints." However, let us mark well that it is up to us where we place our feet. It is our choice of the direction our life goes. If we watch our steps and listen to God, then the psalmist David voices the end results, "The steps of a good man are ordered by the Lord" (Ps. 37:23).

Family Ties

1 Corinthians 12:20 *"But now are they many members, yet but one body."*

Life in Lakeview was certainly not lived in the fast lane. As children we spent most of our time hunting in the woods or playing up near the old brickyard. There were times we tried to catch jack fish in the creek, climb the old beechnut tree, or would spend some time in our home-made-over rowboat down at the lake. Sometimes we would slip some of the Tube Rose snuff from our neighbor's front porch. Once when well hidden in the woods we found that snuff made you sneeze and we thought we had a mouthful of ants. There were times when we had nothing to do but worry our cat. We would take ole Tom and put a piece of tape on his foot. It never hurt him, but the way he boogied and shook when he tried to walk provided many laughs for us.

Now if there was absolutely nothing else we could find to do we would doodle for doodlebugs. This takes a real crafty person. First, you get just the right size straw and then you stick it down into the doodlebug's tunnel. At first he will usually just push it up. Then after a few times of pushing it back down you can lift it out suddenly and bingo—you've got a doodlebug. There's nothing you can really do with a doodlebug. He is just sort of like a roly-poly—you've got him, but what good is he?

Of course, you understand that these times were spent after all of the chores around the house were done. If there was nothing else Mom could find for us to do, she would have us take the sagebrush broom and sweep the dirt in our front yard. There were days when we would spend the early morning hours working in the garden. I loved the taste of fresh green tomatoes and those bright red, hot radishes. In the afternoon we played under the house because it was cool. Our house was built on blocks and if you were not afraid of spiders, then underneath the house was a fun place to be.

Robert and Joe, my two older brothers, loved to tease the rest of us. Sometimes they would try to run off and leave us in some dark part of the woods we did not know very well. This was only for a short period of time and if we just stood still and waited and cried, they would come back for us. In thinking about those old days, I guess one of the most important things to remember is that we were together. Never do I want you to think that we were perfect. There were times of fighting and jealousy and times of telling on each other but, for the major part, we just had fun being with each other. One of the fond memories of childhood is just sitting on the riverbank with my sister, Sue, as she cried over her boyfriend. I remember the sadness in her eyes and I could not understand what it was all about, but I did not like to see my sister cry. We were a family. We liked to be together.

Today, some of us never think of the church as a family. It has become too much like a club or a community organization. We meet together but when the final prayer is said we almost break our necks getting out the door. Have we forgotten that we are a family? When someone in our church is successful do we rejoice with them or are we jealous? When someone in our church is hurting do we weep with them? Paul said in 1 Corinthians, "But now are they many members, yet but one body" (12:20).

My birth family has spread out over many miles, but my spiritual family by birth is very near. Today I will make it a special point to sit down and spend a little more time with my family. I shall not disregard my own wife or children, but today I will enlarge my heart to include some that before were not considered to be a part of the family. Today I will spend some time together with *my family*.

Charlie's Song

Revelation 21:1   *"And I saw a new heaven and a new earth: for the first heaven and the first earth were passed away."*

Old Charlie worked the field next to our house in Lakeview. I am not sure that Charlie was his real name. I do remember his old mule that looked like he had to stand in one place twice to cast a shadow. Charlie lived about a mile from our house, but he worked some of the land that belonged to our Aunt Anna Mae Shields. (We never were sure whether she knew he worked it or not.) Anyway, we spent a lot of time running through his cornfield, but he never once got angry at us. Sometimes we would pause and sit in the shade by the old fence just to listen to his singing and talking to the mule.

Charlie must have been a Christian because nobody sang more about heaven than he did. His black face shining in the boiling sun and his hoarse, rough, bass voice bellowed through the air, "There's a land that is fairer than day, And by faith we can see it afar." I can see him still today trudging along behind the old mule, wearing a torn shirt and overalls so thin you could see his black skin as his legs strained to make each step. Heaven—Old Charlie sure wanted to go to heaven. He loved to talk about heaven. Down through the years many of us have developed some thoughts about heaven that may or may not be very biblical. There are some things that we should keep in mind.

Heaven, as Jesus taught, is first of all a prepared place. Jesus said, "I go to prepare a place for you" (John 14:2). Think of that! Prepared just for me. Most of us live in homes or work in offices that were prepared for someone else, but one day we shall live in a new place prepared just for us.

Secondly, heaven is a promise. Jesus said, "I go and prepare a place for you, I will come again, and receive you unto myself; that where I am, there ye may be also" (v. 3). That, my friend, is a promise. Now, sometimes we as parents make promises to our children and for various reasons cannot fulfill them. However, this promise is bound up in the character of God. Hebrews 10:23 says, "Let us hold fast the profession of our [God]," about whom the writer says in 6:18, "It was impossible for God to lie."

Thirdly, heaven is a person. You know, it really does not matter to me if the streets of heaven are not paved with gold. Heaven is Jesus! "For now we see," as the Bible says, "through a glass, darkly; . . . but then shall I know even as also I am known" (1 Cor. 13:12). We know God today in a unique manner, but one day we will know Him in a complete manner—even as He knows us today.

Fourthly, heaven is a place. When old Charlie talked about heaven he was not speaking of some abstract idea or some concept of perfection. Charlie was speaking of a place.

Several years ago just outside McComb, Mississippi, the pastor and I visited a lady during a revival. While we were there, I quoted the fourteenth chapter of John. When I finished she informed me that I had quoted it wrong because I said rooms instead of mansions. Well, I did not tell her that I had been to seminary and knew Greek and the word used was *abodes,* meaning a place. As we left that home, she stood on the old wood slatted front porch with her snow-white hair flowing in the breeze. She hooked one arm around the white column leaning out toward us then lifted her hand in the air and shouted, "Mansions." I made sure one foot was in the car and raised my arm and returned the shout, "Rooms." Now, we may have had different views on the interpretation but we both agreed that heaven was a place. It was not just a concept of perfection.

There came a day when I walked through the cornfield and it was grown over in weeds. There was no sound of the plow slipping through the soil. No call to the stubborn old mule and no one to stop and pass the time of day with. Charlie did not come to the field one day and we learned later that he had died. Now only the wind whistled through the field and across the hollow to tease my ears, straining to hear once more, "There's a land that is fairer than day. . . ."

Bricks from the Brickyard

Isaiah 48:10   "... I have tested you in the furnace of affliction" (NASB).

As I looked at the large gas valve and small pump I realized that it stood in the same location that Lakeview Baptist Church once stood. Years ago the name of the church had been changed to North 31st and moved into the edge of the ever-growing city of Hattiesburg. As I walked over the old church site nothing seemed right. Even the little creek that once ran near the building was no longer visible.

Soon I had made my way back to the area where some of the broken bricks from the old Hattiesburg Brick Yard used to be thrown. These were the ones that did not stand up under the heat. They were cracked and melted together. Never will I forget that afternoon when we were playing cowboys and Indians in the dirt, clay hills. Claude Malone, one of the boys I was after, rolled a large pile of melted bricks down the hill as I was headed up. The jagged edge of one brick ripped a hole in my leg that still is an ugly scar today. I can remember holding my leg and crying all the way home. Those bricks that should have been used to provide a shelter for someone or to be used in a fireplace had, in fact, become useless. The reason for existence was for good. The problem was they could not stand up under the test of fire. They cracked and broke.

Do you realize our faith is like that? So often I hear people say, "Why did this have to happen to me?" The answer is logical. These things happen to all of us. Often our faith is tested and in the midst of the fire we crack or break. I know it sounds easy to say this from behind a typewriter, but it is also said from experience. There is no way to know if you have faith if it is never tested. Gold and silver must be placed into the furnace before they reach their full value and purity. So we must have those times of suffering, those days of difficulties, the trials and tribulations, if we are to reach our full value and purity.

Let us never forget the Bible says, "It is God which worketh in you both to will and to do of his good pleasure" (Phil. 2:13). Times of suffering need not be a burden, but a blessing. Days of doubts can become days of discovery. Nights of adversities can become a nest of security. The thorns finally gave way to the diadem for Jesus. The old rugged cross was His stepping-stone to the throne of God. So, too, may our times of testing be for us. It is for sure we must not break. Let us not melt any from our own commitment and seek solitude by mingling with others in the brickyard.

On one occasion I asked one of the workers in the yard why some of the bricks cracked and broke. His answer was simple, "Kid, they just could not stand the heat." Can your faith stand the heat? Daniel would have never been the saint he became had he not joined the "lions club." His time in the lions' den and his suffering helped build the saint he became.

Harvesttime

Matthew 13:30　　*"Let both grow together."*

The Mississippi Delta is filled with cotton and soybean farmers. Over the years farmers have learned that weed control is best done by chemicals. Now when I was a boy, whether we were working in our own garden or helping our neighbor we used the old hand method. Perhaps you can remember those days of hoeing cotton or pulling weeds from the garden.

What is amazing to me is that some have taken that same method and applied it to the church. Matthew tells a story where the servants were in agreement with the master. Both wanted to get rid of the tares. Their goal was the same but the conflict came on the method of removal. We all agree that evil should be cast out of the good. We don't want the bad to overcome the good. So many pastors and well-meaning church members often remove folks from their church roll by sending them letters of dismissal. In the country we called this "short benching." Country folks would buy a bench and place it in the church. When they were kicked out, their bench (pew) was removed from the church building. Tare-pulling pastors are still among us. Part of the problem is that we, like the servants, are saying to focus attention on the tares. Pull them up and tear them up. Yet, very often in pulling up the tares we destroy a precious plant growing next to it. It has been my experience in the midst of some tare pulling to see innocent family members hurt and driven out of the church by the cold method of kicking inactive members out.

Some time ago a lady remarked, "I am looking for the perfect church." Now, when she said that, my friend replied, "If you find it don't join it—you will spoil it." He made his point. We all have faults. When we become tare pullers we have assumed the role of God. He alone is the righteous Judge and what is His method of removal? The words of Jesus in this parable are, "Let both grow together unto the harvest." The tares Jesus spoke of were darnel. Darnel is really not a weed but a counterfeit wheat. It grows in most grainfields. Darnel is tall like a wheat shaft. Many call it degenerate wheat. While it is poisonous to man it is not to animals. Jesus said, in essence, to leave it alone. You see, even though we have had nearly two thousand years of preaching the gospel we have not removed sin from one single nation. Indeed, it lies within the best of us. We know sin exists from the courthouse to the church house, from the state department to the children's department and from the heart to the head. We all stand in need of the grace of God constantly. What then shall we do? Oh, let us hear it again, "Let both grow together."

There came a time at our house when it was time to harvest tomatoes. Mom would gather her five children, and off we would go to the garden. I can still remember her bending over holding her apron with one hand and with the other gently removing the tomatoes from the vines. Below the tomato plants were weeds seeking to choke off life, but to no avail. The plants had survived and it was harvesttime. We returned home with our joyous pickings and for days ate fried tomatoes, tomato sandwiches, and tomato gravy. Somewhere I can remember hearing, "Be not overcome of evil, but overcome evil with good" (Rom. 12:21).

The Singing Log

Matthew 15:18   *"But those things which proceed out of the mouth come forth from the heart."*

When childhood days come to mind, one of the most interesting memories I have is the time we spent around the old fireplace. Perhaps you can recall Saturday night with the old washtub pulled up close to the fire. Since there were seven of us and I was next to the youngest, this meant I got out just about as dirty as I got in. You see, we did not change the water in those old tubs. After the bath, I can remember us standing near the fire to warm our bodies so we could offset the cold starched sheets that smelled of pine soap.

How well do I remember that many times we would be sitting around the old fireplace when we would hear this strange sound. If you did not know better, you would have thought a bird was loose in our house. High-pitched sounds bounced around the room as we peered into the magic of the fire. There was an old log on the fire. Dad called this the singing log. Now, not all logs would sing: only those that had years of growth and withstood the elements. Nature had imprisoned in the log those sounds of the forest. That old tree had captured the sound of a morning bird and the frightened cry of animals as danger approached. These sounds of life had been locked deep within the log. Dad had laid an ax to the trunk and after allowing time for it to dry, he placed it on our fire. Once in the heat of the flame, those sounds imprisoned from the forest were released in our presence like a divine concert. Quietly and sweetly that old log sang its heart out. There in the fire, in self-giving sacrifice, the log presented to us a reproduction of what it had locked within long ago.

Mark it well and remember as the old country preacher said, "If your faith fizzles before the finish, it was faulty from the first." As children of God, we need to remember our faith was meant to be tried. Whether it is Shadrach, Meshach, and Abed-nego in the fiery furnace or Daniel standing in the den of lions, when the flames strike, we are to sing.

Imagine if you were standing beside an old saint locked in a dungeon. It is past midnight. Your ankles are swollen and your wrists bleeding from pulling on the chains. You are shut up in prison for preaching the gospel. Old Paul is standing beside you and he leans over and whispers, "Know any songs?" You look at him dazed. "Songs? You must be kidding!" He smiles. "Don't know any, huh?" With that remark he pushes his head upward and says, "This little light of mine, . . . I'm gonna let it shine, this little light of mine, . . . I'm gonna let it shine." There is a brief pause as he looks at you and then with a hoarse sound you start to sing, "This little light of mine." Why, in a matter of minutes, that tune has been picked up by other prisoners and the whole jail is singing, "Let it shine, let it shine, let it shine" (Paul and Silas in jail, Acts 16:19-25).

The devil tempts us to bring us down, but God tests to bring us up. It is through the furnace that we learn what we are really made of. Let me put it to you this way. If your faith has never been tested, how do you know if you have any? Yes, my friend, just like the old log on the fire when we light the flames, what is inside will come out. Vance Havner used to say, "What is in the well comes up in the bucket." Jesus said it this way: "Those things which proceed out of the mouth come forth from the heart" (Matt. 15:18).

Fires of Coal

John 21:9   *"As soon then as they were come to the land, they saw a fire of coals there, and fish laid thereon, and bread."*

As a young lad I spent many happy hours repairing an old boat that someone had abandoned in our community. There were boards to replace and much tar to be spread. I remember that afterwards we also spent many discouraged days drowning worms. I say that because we hardly ever caught any fish. Since then I usually pass up every opportunity I can to go fishing. Now some of my friends are big fishermen. One of my friends, Gordon Fortenberry, tells the story that he once caught a fish that was so big his picture weighed five pounds. Now I can identify with those seven disciples who had fished all night and caught nothing. The Bible says that Jesus instructed them to cast their net on the right side of the boat. When they did they had a large catch. Finally when Peter recognized this was Jesus standing on the shore, he jumped in and swam to meet Him.

Did you ever wonder how Peter felt about the first thing he saw as he walked from the water? The Bible says, "They saw a fire of coals." *Déjà vû* must have ran through his mind. Surely he thought of another fire of coals. Luke tells us in chapter 22: "And when they had kindled a fire in the midst of the hall, and were set down together, Peter sat down among them" (v. 55). This is the scene of his early denial. Three times Peter had vowed that he was not associated with this man called Jesus. Yes, I am sure that Peter remembered and probably sat with his head down during the morning meal. After they had eaten, the Bible says that Jesus addressed Peter. "Simon, son of Jonas," were his words.

Now early in my childhood when my mother really meant business she used my full name. "Gerald Wayne Mixon, you get in this house this very moment." Boy, as long as she said Jerry I knew I could stay out longer, but when she used my real name in a formal way I knew the jig was up! So, I believe Jesus used Simon's formal name to let him know of the severity of the situation. Also, you remember He asked if Simon loved Him. The answer was "Yes, Lord; thou knowest" (John 21:15). Then after each pledge of Peter's love, perhaps for each of his early denials, Jesus recommissioned Simon Peter.

Thank God for a second chance. Jesus was saying, "I know you have failed miserably." But now Peter's default of duty was not to be permanent. In that setting of the fire of coals, Jesus assigned Simon the care of His sheep and lambs. You, my friend, may have failed God in the past, but do not allow defeat to make you a failure. Peter arose from this place to become a great preacher and to write much in the New Testament. Indeed, I like the little poem that goes like this:

> So you made a mistake and regret it
> Well, tell it to God and forget it
> Make your amends, don't dwell on your sin
> For guilt will destroy you if you let it.

All of us got into the kingdom of God by grace and if we continue in it, we will do it by grace. That grace of the second chance was given to Peter and it can be given to you and me. Just as Jesus called for Simon to forget the past and begin again in the present, so He says to us. I like what a radio preacher said, "Remember, if it is not grace, it is not God." So, here is Peter, forgiven and reinstated. Jesus asked him to translate his love for Him from words to ministry. Jesus said, "Feed my sheep" (John 21:16-17). When Peter had failed, he went back to the old life. He went fishing. However, the grace that saved him now was willing to trust to him again the care of Jesus' little children. It was in this setting that Peter's ministry continued as it had begun beside a fishing boat three years earlier. And after this Jesus said to Peter, "Follow me" (v. 19).

Mississippi Mud House

Matthew 7:24

"Whosoever heareth . . . I will liken him unto a wise man which built his house upon a rock."

One of our favorite games of childhood when we were not building huts in the woods was to play in the red clay hills and the good old Mississippi mud. Behind Lakeview Baptist Church was a section of land where the water ran down the brickyard hill and into low land. The dirt there was a mixture of sand and clay. We used to enjoy hours of fun making bricks out of the clay. We could make a pretty good brick with a mixture of the sand and clay. The ground was usually wet because of the water flowing from above. After making our bricks we used a long board borrowed from some neighbor who was not at home. The bricks were placed on this board and allowed to dry in the sun for a couple of days. The next step was to prepare a thin mixture of the same mud and water (without the sand) for a mortar. When all of this was ready, we would build a house. I cannot tell you how many times we built and rebuilt our house. It seemed as though it was a thousand times. The problem was that it would stand only for a couple of days or at least until it rained. Most of the problem was in the fact that I did not know you were supposed to lay a foundation.

Somewhere I read that Frank Lloyd Wright built the Imperial Hotel in Tokyo. In this beautiful land of earthquakes and tremors this hotel has stood. The reason is simple. About eight feet beneath the earth's surface Mr. Wright discovered a sixty-foot bed of soft mud. When buildings around the hotel crumbled and fell, this building stood. The foundation was actually floating on the bed of mud that acted as a shock absorber.

If you study the life of trees you will notice those that stand are not the ones with big limbs and branches. The trees that weather the storms are the ones who have developed their roots.

There is a sure promise to all of us. The winds are coming. Jesus said it this way, "Whosoever heareth . . . I will liken him unto a wise man, which built his house upon a rock." Then He spoke of the foolish man saying, "Every one that heareth these sayings of mine, and doeth them not, shall be likened unto a foolish man, which built his house upon the sand." Then at the conclusion of both statements Jesus had this to say: "The rain descended, and the floods came, and the winds blew and beat upon that house" (vv. 25-26). Folks, the wind, the rain, the floods are coming. The question we must ask is, "Will our house stand in the storms of life?" If it stands it will be because of the solid foundation. When our life crumbles, it will be because of the foundation.

There is a solid gold foundation for the gate of the Fortress of Purandhar, India. The rajah of Bihar built it in 1290. The foundation is a 35-foot square which measures 12 feet deep. The foundation contains 50,000 gold bricks weighing 4,320 grains each. Experts had said no foundation would hold any structure on this marshy ground. The gate still stands today (1987).

There is a connection between saying and doing or, as stated by Jesus, hearing and doing. The one who hears His word and does it will build his house (life) upon a solid foundation. The Old Testament psalmist said, "Blessed is the man who walketh not in the counsel of the ungodly. . . . He shall be like a tree planted . . . that bringeth forth his fruit . . . his leaf also shall not wither" (Ps. 1:1-3). As a child I built on a poor foundation, but thank goodness when "I became a man I put away childish things."

Can You Take a Dare?

Philippians 1:14   *"And many of the brethren in the Lord . . . are much more bold to speak the word without fear."*

What were some of the daring events of your youth? I remember we used to see who could walk the longest on the hot railroad tracks at noon with their bare feet. Sometimes we would hang underneath the trestle by our hands and watch the freight train pass above. Or we would see who would drink from the muddiest pond or stand around on the riverbank daring each other to be the first one in. Many were the times we tried to see who could climb the highest in a tree. One of the games we played that was fun was to see who could ride pine saplings nearest to the ground. You had to pick one that was tall and skinny but one you could climb to the very top. Once a tree broke with my brother, Joe, and he hit the ground in a squatting position. He was so stove up he could not move. I am not kidding, we carried him all the way home in that squatting position. He looked like Chief Sitting Bull. As life would go for Joe, nothing was broken and after we managed to get his nose away from his toes, life smelled better to him.

Late in the afternoon when the tin roofs cooled we

would take an old feed sack and slide down the top section of an old house. Actually, it was the house Uncle Carl and Aunt C. C. lived in. It was some trick to catch a limb from a nearby tree to keep from going off the roof. If there was nothing else we could think of, we tried to see who could get the closest to Mr. Malone's bull. It took a lot of nerve to run up to that big joker, slap him on the backside, and then run back to the fence. Daring events such as this not only made our hearts beat fast, but they provided some entertainment for otherwise dull summer days. I don't know about you, but I have never been much on letting a dare go to waste. If someone said, "I dare you," he could get me to do most anything.

The dictionary says that to dare means to challenge or to venture to do something that takes courage. Some of our early childhood dares did not take courage so much as the lack of common sense. One of the prayers of my life is that I can have that same courage of my foolish youth translated into boldness in my spiritual life. In other words, to be like those folks Paul spoke of in Philippians when he said, "And many of the brethren in the Lord, waxing confident by my bonds, are much more bold to speak the word without fear." You know, most of us still have trouble speaking out for the Lord. We still have the idea that we do not want to offend someone or drive them away from God. As one evangelist said, "Where are you going to drive them? To hell number two? If they are away from God and lost, then they cannot get any farther away." Yet we all have a certain amount of fear about speaking out for Jesus.

A certain amount of fear is great. We need to be cautious and considerate about how and when we speak for the Lord. Yes, we do need to witness, but ways and words need to be carefully chosen. While I want to be bold in the

Lord, I never want to be rude. I want to be daring, but never damaging. One rule of thumb I have tried to use is when I have the opportunity to give a witness, no matter how small it may seem, I do so with the assurance that it is not my ability but His Word that is important. I want every day to see every opportunity as a challenge to speak a word about Him, being careful and cautious. Maybe you could try this approach. I dare you!

The Way Home

Psalm 1:1-2   *"Blessed is the man that walketh not in the counsel of the ungodly. . . . His delight is in the law of the Lord."*

During the days of my full-time evangelism, we lived in Castle Manor Estates in the city of Petal, Mississippi. It was a very cold winter day and we needed some wood to start a fire in our new fireplace. Rick Miller, son of Richard and Jean Miller, a full-time music team I sometimes traveled with, was staying with us for a few days. Over to the right and back deep in the woods I knew of an old fence row that had some dry pine poles that had broken off even with the ground. These old posts I knew would make excellent wood to start our fire with. So, with hatchet in hand, Rick, my six-year-old son, Jeff, and I made our way deep into the forest. Can you believe that after we found the posts and started home, we discovered that we were lost! Never in a million years could you have convinced me that you could get me lost in those woods. However, it was late in the evening, and in the dark all of the woods looked the same. I pushed back bushes and stumbled around for almost an hour before I admitted I did not know where we were or which way to go. Rick finally admitted he was lost, too.

As we stood there listening to see if we could hear an auto on the nearby highway, Jeff caught my eye. Up to this point, he had followed my instructions and stayed right behind us. He never did question the way I was leading, but now he looked as though he had something to say. Jeff pointed toward a tree leaning over against another and said, "That is the way home, Dad." Rick looked at me and said to Jeff, "Are you sure that is the way home?" "Yep," Jeff said, and started walking toward the leaning tree. Can you believe that the both of us fell in right behind my six-year-old and marched just like we knew where we were going. After we made it back to the main road, dragging our two fence posts, we instructed Jeff to say *nothing* about being lost. He did not seem to understand what being lost meant, but we hoped he did!

Have you ever been lost downtown? It is a feeling that is not pleasant. Whether in the woods or right in the center of a big shopping mall, it is a feeling that is not well received. During this time nothing seems right. Everything seems upside down. We all need to remember that we are on a journey in this life. There are times when we take a side street. Often we are on a detour road because of anger, hate, greed, and in some cases just plain laziness.

Some of our church members are lost in discouragement and many are lost in sin. What happens when a Christian is lost? Now, I do not mean lost and going to hell, but lost their way. They have become dead to good works. What happens when you as a Christian feel this way? Let me suggest that you do what Jeff did. Look for something familiar. You see, the reason Jeff could lead us out was because he found a familiar object that showed him the way home. Jeff knew about the leaning tree. It is an old saying, but very true. We must return to daily Bible reading and times of personal prayer when we have lost our way as a child of God. There is no way we can find our way back to fellowship with God unless we look into His Word. There is one thing for sure about something we lose. Mom used to say, "Jerry, you will find it right where you left it." She was right. You will find God right where you left Him. He never leaves us. Oh, it seems as though He has, but that is just our feeling. When we get alone with the Word and with Him we soon find, as the songwriter said, "He was there all the time."

You will find it true that often success leads us off track. Right in the middle of success we pop our wheels and take off down the road of pride, and, bang, we feel lost again. The feeling of being lost is a time of no fruit bearing in our life. Let each of us today find those markings, those familiar guideposts of Bible reading and prayer along with confession and forgiveness of others. When we have looked to these age-old guidelines, we will be slipping through the darkness and we will arrive safe with our treasure from the forest.

Squirrel Hunting

Luke 18:7 *"And shall not God avenge his own elect, which cry day and night unto him?"*

The community of Goss is located about eight miles out of Columbia, Mississippi. Goss Baptist Church called me as their pastor and I served with them for five years. It was during that time that J. B. Ivey invited me to go squirrel hunting with him. After we had hunted all morning we had not killed one squirrel. His dog had treed time and time again. We would shake the tree, but still no squirrel. When it was close to lunch, we started back toward home and I was giving J. B. a hard time about his dog. As we were walking, J. B. remarked that we had not seen the dog for sometime now. Well, as far as I was concerned, I did not care if we ever saw that lying squirrel dog again.

Then it happened, and I say some of you will not believe this, but that dog came out of the bushes and stood directly in front of us. Both of us stopped dead still. Pooch had something in his mouth. Then the dog walked up to us and laid a big red squirrel at our feet. As we stood in amazement, Pooch walked off a few yards and laid down in the shade. I said, "J. B., do you know what that dog is telling you?" J. B. said, "Yeah, he is saying, "Fellows, this is what we are looking for, this is what a squirrel looks like." I could not believe it. That dog thought we were blind. He was very unusual, but so was J. B. Ivey.

Pooch taught us a lesson that day by showing us what we were looking for. Some of the teachings of Jesus are along this line. Jesus would say the Word of God is like this, and He would proceed to tell about a farmer who sowed his seed in the field. The harvest was not dependent on how good a farmer he was, but rather on the condition of the soil. Again He said that the love of God is like the love the father had for the prodigal son. When the son came home he found a loving, forgiving father. Jesus said in effect that God is like that. These are what we call comparison parables. He says this is like that. The kingdom of heaven is like a grain of mustard seed. It starts out small but becomes very large. You see, these are comparison parables. These are rather easily understood.

There are three parables of Jesus that do not fall in this category. They are the parable of the friend at midnight (Luke 11:5), the unjust steward (Luke 16:1), and the judge who feared not God (Luke 18:2). If you follow the comparison theory, is Jesus saying to act like the unjust steward? Does the end justify the means? Is He saying the man will rise from his bed, give you a loaf of bread because he wants to be left alone? Is God like that? Of course not; these are comparison parables by *contrast*.

Jesus wants us to hear Him say that if your neighbor will give you bread because you kept knocking, how much more will God answer if you keep praying. Jesus is saying if an evil, unjust steward can use wealth to secure his future, how much more should we as the people of God use wealth to secure the lives of others. Jesus is saying if an unjust judge who respects neither man nor God will give in, how much more will our "God avenge his own elect, which cry day and night unto him?" (Luke 18:7*b*). God often may teach us by comparison, but He will also in the midst of the comparison sometimes teach us by contrast, saying if we "being evil, know how to give good gifts unto your children, how much more shall your [HEAVENLY] Father . . . give good things to them that ask?" (Luke 7:11).

This is an important lesson from Luke 11 and Luke 18: It is a matter of never losing hope in prayer. Do not stop praying. These parables may have been given to teach us more about ourselves than about God. You see, we are often prone to lose hope. If our prayers are not answered, we feel as though God is the unrighteous judge. But looking back, can't you thank God for some of the prayers He did not answer? Let these comparison-by-contrast parables cause you once again to renew your faith in a God who answers prayer. This would be a good time to bow your head and pray right now. Let's pray!

On the Road Again

Hebrews 13:21 *"Make you perfect in every good work to do his will."*

In August 1982 we moved from Goss Baptist Church, Columbia, Mississippi, to the First Baptist Church of Winona, Mississippi. The move was a difficult one for me as well as my family. There were so many wonderful people in Goss Baptist Church that we really hated to leave. They had been so kind and loving to all of us. The year before they had given us a new 1981 Pontiac on Valentine's Day. While I really wanted to stay in the comfort zone of that church, I felt it was God's will for us to move to the north hill country of Mississippi.

Perhaps the mood of it all is best expressed in a letter written by my ten-year-old daughter, Lanay:

> Me and my friend, Angela, had gotten to be really close friends. One day my father told me we were going to move to another town. I was really sad about moving. I liked that place. My father was a preacher, so I had to go. It was our last Sunday at Goss Baptist Church and the church was giving a dinner in the Family Life Center for us. After we ate, my mother

and me were both crying about moving. We were hugging everybody and saying good-bye. The next day was Monday and I was going to swim at the pool. I had to really swim, because it was my last day till moving time. I got sadder. On Tuesday, it was time to move. Then I was really sad. We were moving to Winona, Mississippi. It was a little town. When we got there we had to unpack everything. I had a little room. The house was small, but it would do for me, I said. Then it was time to make friends. I made friends with Margaret, Renee, Lynn, Michele, Libby, and a whole lot of people at the church. It was time to go to school again. I was scared because now I would have to make new friends at school too. I was scared the first day, but I went on. People thought I had failed and was supposed to be in the 8th grade because I was so tall. They called me a flunker. That made me mad! Then they called me "long nose" because I have a big nose. I was really embarrassed but I did not care. As the days went on, the 5th grade got better. I met a lot of people. My favorite teacher is Mrs. Alford. She is really nice and pretty. I was in level two, but after six weeks I got moved up to level one (the highest level). I really hated living in this new town, but it got better. One day (at school) we had homecoming and I got homecoming queen. I still write all my friends in Columbia and they write me. Sometimes they come to see us. I miss everyone in Goss so I want them to read this sentence, "Even though we are not in the same town we can still love each other the same."

I love you,
LANAY MIXON

When we follow God's will for our lives, it may not always be easy, but it will always be best. I am happy to report that while we made new friends, we did not lose old friends. We soon found that people everywhere are the same when they have Christ in their lives. Should you be making some decision in your life that will affect the family? Remember, "God gives the best to those who leave the choice with Him."

Cat in the Box

John 8:44   *"The devil . . . is a liar, and the father of it."*

    Several years ago while attending a youth retreat I heard P. A. "Red" Michel tell the story of a lady who accidentally ran over a cat. After going from house to house, she finally located the owner. After she explained that it was an accident she asked if there was something she could do. The lady of the house suggested that she might help her dispose of the animal before her daughter came home from school. An old shoe box was given to her and after placing the cat in the box, she laid it on the floor of the passenger's side of the car. Her intentions were to drop it in the first garbage disposal she found. She turned the radio on to soothe her nerves, and before she realized it she was at the shopping center. Being late for her shopping spree, she hurried toward the entrance and then remembered the cat in the box on the floor of her automobile.

    As she turned to go back to her car, she saw a lady looking in the car window. *Now, what is she looking at,* she thought. *There is nothing in there. Oh, no, you don't suppose she thinks, she couldn't and besides, she wouldn't. I mean, surely she is not going to steal what she thinks is a new pair of shoes?* At that moment the lady opened the car door and picked up the box. Would you believe she came straight toward the entrance? The car owner followed her into the coffee shop and sat at the table next to her. When the lady could stand it no longer, she opened the box to see her new pair of shoes. "Ohoooooo," she screamed and fainted! The management thought she had a heart attack and called the emergency medical team. When the ambulance arrived and as they put her on the stretcher, the lady who had run over the cat walked over and placed the shoe box on the stretcher and remarked, "Don't forget her new pair of shoes."

If there is one thing I have learned in life it is that you cannot trust the devil. The Bible says he is a liar and has been so from the beginning (John 8:44). You can never believe what the devil says. As one famous evangelist says, "He will tell you about the kick, but not the kick back. He will speak of the thrill, but never tell you that sin kills. He will talk about the fascination of sin, but never the assassination." You see, he is a liar and the father of all lies. Not long ago I heard a pastor say, "We are never more like the devil than when we lie." There is absolutely no truth in him. Even when he quotes the Bible you had better watch out, because he will abuse and misuse it. Do you really think he could have led the prodigal son into the far country if he had shown him the finished product—if he had given him a picture of himself sitting on the pigpen fence of life shucking corn to feed the hogs? No! Why, the prodigal would have never left home. Instead, the devil painted a beautiful picture of the far country. He lied!

Oh, how do we all need to remember the carpet always looks cleaner in the home of someone else. The devil will make us all sorts of promises. He will promise a new pair of shoes, but we will wind up with an old dead cat!

Someone in the Stands

Luke 15:10   *"There is joy in the presence
of the angels of God over
one sinner that repenteth."*

Johnny was worried about his father. Word had come to him at school that his father had been taken to the hospital. Later, as he arrived in the emergency room he was greeted by a host of people who tried their best to console him. His dad had died en route to the hospital. Later in the afternoon, the football coach and most of the players assured Johnny that they did not expect him to play in the championship game that evening. After listening to their argument, Johnny replied, "Coach, this will be the first time Dad will see me play. I really think I should play tonight." You see, Johnny's father had been born blind.

Now I know the story is very touching, but is it scriptural? If we think that folks who die and go to be with the Lord spend their time watching what is happening here on earth, we simply listen to tradition rather than the Word of God. Yes, I know it sounds right, but even in theory it is not practical. Suppose a lady who lost her husband is about to be remarried. Do you suppose that God would allow her former husband to view her wedding night? Here is a lad whose blind father dies and his first day in heaven he wants to sit and watch a football game here on earth. Think of some godly mother who dies and then for the next twenty or so years she views the tragic life of her children here on earth.

I say again, it is not even logical for us to assume God would allow those in heaven to view what is happening here on earth. We must give God credit for better sense than we have, at least. God would not allow one piece of news from this earth to enter heaven and spoil our abode with Him. There is, however, some news that gets into heaven. I do not mean to say that folks up there are viewing what is going on down here, but I can assure you every time the angelic chorus strikes up a praise song—well, folks in heaven know that somebody here on earth just got saved. "I say unto you, there is joy in the presence of angels of God over one sinner that repenteth" (Luke 15:10). Let us remember the only news that gets into heaven is salvation news.

Many would have us believe otherwise and some on the basis of Hebrews 12:1 which states, "Seeing we also are compassed about with so great a cloud of witnesses. . . ." But this verse does not mean that those in heaven view what is going on here on earth. Just suppose you are a football player and at halftime, with your team behind by two touchdowns, you sit exhausted in the locker room. The coach walks in and announces that Bart Starr has just arrived in the stands. Someone else comes in and says a bus just brought in Walter Peyton, Archie Manning, Ray Perkins, Raymond Berry, and Joe Namath. I can assure you that because of those who are now sitting in the stands, you would play a better ball game the second half. You see, you would be inspired by those who were in the stands. They inspire you! This is what the writer of Hebrews is saying. We should be inspired to lay aside all the weights and sins that trip and drag us down, remembering Moses and Elijah and others who have paved the way—those great champions of the faith he had just listed in Hebrews 11—people like Jacob, Joseph, Enoch, Abraham, Noah, Rahab, Samson, and David. These all died clinging, climbing, and claiming the faith and they by example inspire us. Let us understand it is not what the people in the grandstands see that inspire us. It is who we see in the grandstands that challenges us to continue toward the prize that has been set before us.

Does God Play Fair?

Matthew 25:29

"For unto every one that hath shall be given, and he shall have abundance: but from him that hath not shall be taken away even that which he hath."

Early childhood days brought many hours of playful games. Sometimes it was "Hide and Seek," "Mother, May I?" or some other homemade game. It never failed that before the game was up, someone would cry out, "Play fair." This would always embark us on a spree of yells, "You cheated," followed by, "I did not!" This was repeated several times and then Mother would step to the door and shout, "You kids better play fair or I will stop the play right this instant."

Have you ever wanted to say that to God? Well, I guess most of us have whether we admit it or not. Life is not fair, but, after all, who promised us it would be? We live in a corrupt world and sometimes even the good guys don't play fair. Yet, with all of this in mind, it would seem that God, above all, would play fair with us. However, at the first reading of this passage it would seem that we have the right to cry, "Foul." I mean if you are going to take from the guy who has and give to the guy who has not, then hooray for Robin Hood! God, on the other hand, sometimes seems to do just the opposite. If charities did that we certainly would not give to them.

If you read this parable you will find several things worth consideration. First, no servant in this story was without a calling or without capital. They all had been given a means and a measurement. They had a business and a wherewith to do business. So, let us not consider God unfair. You know, each one of us has been given the capacity for rendering some service to help a poor world. God has given us all an ability. Secondly, each did not receive the same gift. There was a vast difference in the ability and the opportunity for each servant.

We have neither the right nor the obligation to expect pastors and church members to express their ministry in the same manner. Nevertheless, often we deem one greater or more committed than the other because either his gift is more or his opportunity for expressing it is greater. I think the point is that all have an endowment and whether it be small or large makes no difference. All of our gifts are grace gifts, so there is no cause for strutting. If our talent is only one, there is equally no cause for discouragement. With a careful reading you can see that this man was very content until he began comparing his gift with others. Often we feel unworthy because we cannot sing a beautiful solo or preach a masterful sermon.

Listen folks, it matters not what we have been given, but what really counts is what we do with what we have. Be it one talent or five, we must not bury our grace gift. All of us will be far richer when we learn that God will not judge us by the way we use what we do not possess. But He will judge us by the use we make of the gifts that are actually our own. This puts us all on equal ground.

As you read this parable, remember that when the accounting came there was no question about popularity, no asking of position, and no seeking of information about where they served. On the basis of the servants' answers, the only question asked seemed to have been, "What did you do with what I gave you?" It is a matter of how faithful you have been with what you had. Now, that is a valid question for each of us no matter what kind or how many talents we possess. Each servant was commended if he had been faithful, if he had used what he had been given. Rewards were then determined on the basis of faithfulness. Those who would cry unfair have not taken the time to read or to understand the principle.

It is true in life that if you do not use your arm you will lose the use of it. If we do not use it, we lose it. Each person in the story had the opportunity to do his best. Each of us has that same opportunity, whether it be giving a cool drink of water or giving our life in the foreign mision service. God has the ability to rate each the same if they are our best. I have come to the conclusion that when we have given God our best He rates it as perfection. In the area of Christian service under His leadership when you have done all He has asked you to do, there is nothing more to be added. That is perfection!

One does not have to beat his wife to destroy a marriage, just neglect her. You do not lose a friend by something you say; it is usually because you say nothing. "Use it or lose it" seems to be the principle that God works under here. When we consider our abilities in the light of this passage, we shall look to God and do our best. We shall never feel proud of what we do or discouraged because others do more. Indeed, we shall never in light of this cry out to God saying, "Play fair!"

Creed or Confidence

Job 23:10   *"When he hath tried me, I shall come forth as gold."*

What if everything you had been taught about God was suddenly destroyed? If your faith proved to be in error, could you still trust God? This happened to a man in the Bible named Job. The basic theology of God during those days was that if a man was righteous, God would bless him. The other side of the coin was that if a man was bad, God would punish him. During his lifetime, Job lost his children, his wealth, and his health. It seemed as though a good God had turned bad. Job's concept that the righteous would prosper and the wicked would suffer rose to the question, "Why do the righteous suffer and the wicked prosper?" Everything Job knew about God was destroyed. In reality his creed was gone! What would you do if everything you believed about God was suddenly destroyed? Hear the words of Job, "When he hath tried me, I shall come forth as gold" (Job 23:10). Job's creed was gone, but his faith was strong. Job still trusted God.

Now, you and I have an advantage that Job did not have. We understand that the devil was attacking Job by God's permission. You see, Job was righteous and the devil hates righteousness. God loves righteousness and He wanted Job to become more righteous. If you were to blow a balloon up full of air it would be full, but if you blew harder it would be fuller still. It was perfectly full, but you made it fuller. The Bible even declares that Jesus was perfect, yet became more perfect through suffering (Heb. 5:8). The devil thought by his attack on Job he would destroy righteousness, but God knew that it would make Job more righteous. God knew He could trust Job through suffering. Can God trust us to suffer? Can God rely on our suffering to drive us to Him or from Him? Job even came to the place that he said, "Though he slay me, yet will I trust in him" (Job 13:15).

Sometimes I have heard people discuss the life of Job and say that he suffered because of some secret sin. Could we set the record straight here? What Job suffered was not the direct or indirect results of his sin or the sin of anyone else. Listen to the reason God gives for Job's suffering. "There is no one like him on the earth; a blameless and upright man fearing God and turning away from evil. And he still holds fast his integrity, although you [SATAN] incited Me [GOD] against him [JOB], to ruin him [JOB] without cause" (Job 2:3, NASB). Hear from the lips of our God that the suffering of Job came not because he had sinned. He suffered because he was righteous.

Job came to the place that is expressed in chapter 23 where he could not find God anywhere. If he looked to the east or west, God was simply not there. Has there been that kind of midnight in your experience? Have there been times when you just could not smell, taste, touch, see, or hear God, and still you trusted Him? Job came to that place and lost his creed, but not his confidence in God. I love to read the last chapter of Job, for it is here that we understand the reason for his suffering. Job cries out, "My ears have heard of you, but now my eyes have seen you" (Job 42:5, author's words).

In his suffering Job, even when he could not find God, learned more about God. You see, he repented, but it was a repentance of thinking he could understand his suffering if God would explain it. In essence, God said in chapter 41 that if Job could not understand the things that are, what made him think he could understand things that should be? God was saying no explanation was needed and if He did explain Job could not understand. So hear again Job crying out, "I have uttered things I did not understand, things too wonderful for me, which I did not know" (Job 42:3, RSV). One of the reasons a righteous person suffers is because he is righteous. God knows He can trust us, but the question remains whether we are willing to trust Him.

God Loves Jesus

John 5:20   *"For the Father loveth the Son."*

In Lakeview Baptist Church one of the first songs we learned to sing was "Jesus Loves Me." It was here that God captured my soul, with the concept that God could love me. Through the years most of us have faced the loss of loved ones or some other tragic situation where we questioned, If God loved us, why would He allow this to happen? You see, "Jesus loves me" is a good place to start with God, but you do not want to stay there. There is someone that God loves even more than He loves us. John says, "The Father loveth the Son."

When we understand that this world does not operate around us but around the Father's love for His Son, then we have moved from the God-bless-me area to the God-bless-Jesus area. However, most Christians are content to live out their Christian experience, never moving from the God-bless-me syndrome. As long as we live in this concept we never can explain the death of a child, the bankruptcy of a business, or any other tragedy. On the other hand, if we understand that God has built a world and planned it around His Son instead of us, then we are on our way. You see, years ago God decided to have a world filled with people who would love His Son just as He loves His Son. He built this world so that His Son would be the center of everything. Indeed, He would be the glue that held it all together. He made it so that if we are to have anything in the spiritual life, we would have it through His Son. God so ordered that if anyone was to come to know Him they would have to come through His Son.

You can go to any book in the world and if you could contain all of the knowledge of man, you could put it between the A and the Z. God says that Jesus is the Alpha and the Omega, the beginning and the end. In other words, nothing before Him, nothing after Him, and everything is with Him. Let me say it this way: When you move up to the God-loves-Jesus plateau instead of the God-bless-me, you will receive more blessings by accident than you could ever have through begging and pleading. I have never known a mother who, if you honored her son or daughter, would not also honor you. It is even so with God. If you, my dear friend, will stop asking God to bless you, stop thinking that this world revolves around you, and start honoring His Son, Jesus Christ, God will bless you so much that you will be amazed.

What Is Above God's Name?

Psalm 138:2 *"Thou has magnified thy word above thy name."*

Many of you will remember that in days gone by the old folks used to say a man's word was his bond. Now, they are saying that if a man told you something you could depend on it. Homer Huggins lived across the gravel road from us in Lakeview. One of his favorite expressions was, "If I tell you a chicken dips snuff—just look under her wing and you will find a can." Homer, like most of the older people, considered his word very important. However, we live today in an age of contracts, lawyers, and lawsuits because the average Americans no longer can trust each other.

In our spiritual lives we have disagreement among the brethren today on the validity of God's Word. Not too long ago I came across a verse while reading the Psalms that shook me to my bones. You know there have been many important names in history, but none so important as the name of Jesus. The Bible says that His name is above the name of all others. Jesus is a name given by God Himself, but there is something that God has magnified even above the name of Jesus. You say, What? Right, same reaction I had when I first read the verse. Now, I am sure

What Is Above God's Name?

I had read it before but for some reason it did not register. Listen to what the writer of Psalm 138 says, "For thou has magnified thy word above all thy name" (v. 2). Hey, He did not just magnify something above the name of Jesus, He magnified it above the name of God himself. What is this great magnification? It is His Word! God has placed His Word even above His own name. Can we not see the value that God has placed on His Word?

I have a friend who has been close to me over the years. He is a great guy and fun to be around. He is moral and well-meaning in all that he does, but he has one flaw. He will promise you the moon. Oh, he means well, but he just has the habit of saying he can when he cannot. He may have every intention of doing what he says, but the fact is most folks have lost their confidence in him because he always promises more than he is able to deliver.

God is not like that! You see, God knows that if you cannot trust a man's word you cannot trust the man. So God has magnified His Word even above His name—not at the expense of His name, but to honor His Word in such a way that His name will be a name you can trust.

When I read this verse and let it sink deep into my spirit, it gave a new meaning to every promise I read in the Bible. You see, back behind this promise is the great name of God. He knows that if I can trust His Word, if I can believe what He says, I can trust Him. He has the power and the person, the resources and restraint, the means and the measure, the time and the treasure, the will and the way to fulfill each pledge made in His Word because He has magnified it even above His own name. A country preacher friend put it this way: "What He says, He will do and what He does, He said He would."

My Mad Mirror

Ephesians 4:26 *"Let not the sun go down upon your wrath."*

She walked up to me right after the sermon and said, "Preacher, I want to give you a piece of my mind." Well, I was not sure she could spare it, but I let her explode anyway. "I am so mad I could bite your head off," she shouted. Looking back on the situation, if she had, she would have had more brains in her stomach than she had in her head. Most of us never get around to realizing that when we lose our cool—and most of us have at one time or another—we not only hurt others but we hurt ourselves.

The Bible gives us the concept that we should never go to bed mad. You know, when you put the body to bed, but the mind decides to stay up all night. Oh, you may even close your eyes and drift into a slumber, but you never rest. All night long little militant men and poison paratroopers invade your room. Waves of anxiety bombard your system like darts, and in the morning you rise worse off than you were before you went to bed. What happened? Very simple: Your body lay down, but your mind never did. Anger can rob you not only of your spiritual joy but also of your sleep.

The Bible says we are not to let the sun go down on our wrath. This does not only apply when we are mad at others but also when we are just plain mad. Sometimes we are mad at ourselves, at God, or even at the dog. We need to bury the hatchet before we bury the body in bed.

You know, some husbands and wives never fight. Why, they have such a wonderful relationship, they just never have a cross word. Vicki and I have been married eighteen years. Now, in those eighteen years, we have never gone to bed one time mad. Can you believe that? I mean, not one time did we lay the body down and keep the mind up. We never went to bed mad. However, there were some times we just stayed up all night. Your marriage may be one of those perfect ones and, if so, I am proud for you, but if it is like most of us you are going to have to find some way to ease the burden before bed or you will not sleep.

One man told me that when he and his wife had a fuss he would always take a walk to cool down. I could tell by his tan he spent a lot of time walking. Some folks say pray, but I have a difficult time praying when I am mad. You might think that is the time to pray, but I do not.

"Well, then, Brother Jerry, what do you do?" Remember, what works for me may also work for you. The first thing I do is hold my tongue. I bite my tongue so I won't have to eat my words later. The second thing I do is get alone. Now, the only place in my house to be alone is the bathroom. Guess what I do next? I look in the mirror. There alone, looking in the mirror at myself, I usually see tight lips, eyes full of darts, and a frown. The longer I stare at myself the more of myself I see. What I see I do not like. After a while I begin to think this is rather silly. In the other room is a woman or child who loves me very much.

I have been rather selfish. Once I am calm and have a smile, I pray. Then after the prayer I usually go help my wife do something. At first, we do not talk, but later I will say I am sorry and we start over.

James said, "If any be a hearer of the word, and not a doer, he is like unto a man beholding his natural face in a glass: For he beholdeth himself, and goeth his way and . . . forgetteth" (Jas. 1:23-24). A nice, long look at myself helps me see what God wants to change in me. Anger is always the first to go.

The White Suit

2 Corinthians 3:9 *"Much more doth the ministration of righteousness exceed in glory."*

Most of us have grown up under the impact of being rewarded for good. Because of this we have responded in the Christian experience much the same way. We want to be rewarded when we are good. However, the Christian life began in grace and continues in grace. You have just as much of the grace of God available to you on the day you kicked the cat and cussed the dog as the day you read your Bible and prayed three times. You see, grace is outside the area of performance. The God of the New Testament comes to you when you sin with the face of grace, not of revenge. He comes wanting to forgive. In truth, He comes forgiving. All that you have as a child of God comes from your being in Christ, not your performance for Christ.

We are standing in the arena of grace, not performance. What we do or do not do each day does not move us closer or drive us farther from God. Our standing with Him is that we are His children. Now, when we sin or when we are not doing what God will have us do, there will be a sense of failure in our lives. We will feel at a distance from

God, but that is a simple emotion. The fact is we are still in the area of grace. Our fellowship with God has been broken, but not our relationship. We will lose that sense of the awareness of the presence of God. Then when we have confessed that sin and the channel of forgiveness flows freely, we will once again feel His presence.

The devil is always trying to get us in the area of self-righteousness. I am better than you because I read the Bible daily or I go soul-winning or do some Christian ritual. However, the New Testament calls our new standing in Christ a "ministry of righteousness" (2 Cor. 3:9, NASB). Folks, this means God has declared us right with Him and that was by grace through His Son, Jesus Christ. When we sin the devil says, "See there, you are not worthy; how could a Christian do that?" When he gets you there you are living with one foot in the Old Testament and one in the New Testament. Notice I am saying when we sin, not if we sin, we should confess it immediately.

I am sure that some of you are saying, "This is my kind of preacher. He is saying you just get saved and live like you want to." No, I am saying that we have been saved by the grace of God and we are kept saved by the grace of God. This is not a performance test. I do not have to live up to anything. You see, most of us have never come to realize who we are in Christ. Let me express it the way I heard Peter Lord explain: "Knowing who we are in Jesus." He said, "How much of you does God approve of right now?" One might reply, "About 40 percent or maybe 75 percent on a good day." I have good news for you. God approves of you 100 percent. In the day you received Jesus into your heart you were "accepted in the beloved" (Eph. 1:6).

Just suppose you went to work in a service station in a white suit and I showed up in blue jeans. The boss came out and smeared oil on your white suit and on my jeans. Well, my jeans were already dirty so one more speck would not matter, but you, goodness, you would have a fit if one drop of oil got on your pretty white suit. Right—the application is simple. Knowing who we are in Christ will not give us free rein to sin, but will give us the freedom to walk in grace. Most of us have been told we are dirty, rotten, filthy sinners so long or we have so much sin in our lives that one more drop of oil will not hurt. Yet, if we realize that God accepts us in Jesus, proclaims us perfect, and dresses us in the white righteousness of Jesus, I tell you we will approach each day not wanting to have a speck of sin to blot the beautiful white suit of Jesus that we wear.

Don't Rain on My Parade

Matthew 5:13 *"Ye are the salt of the earth."*

You know, folks are usually down on what they are not up on, but most of the time we all feel like we are a "day late and a dollar short." Feelings have a way of coming and going, thank the Lord. We can feel lower than a snake one minute and sky high the next. Sometimes our feelings change with the weather. If it is cloudy, we are moody blue and when the sun is shining, we perk up. Bad news gets us down, but good news picks us up. You know, down through the years I have found that some people change us when they are around. I remember once my mother went to visit a neighbor in the hospital and while she was there she became ill and had to spend a couple of days there herself.

The following day I was visiting her when a deacon came in from my church. After talking for a few minutes, he said, "Mrs. Mixon, I had a friend that got sick and that night he died." Now, you can believe I ushered him out of the room immediately. He did not bring sunshine; he brought rain. People can do wonders for feelings with just a few words. You wear a new outfit or a new hairstyle and folks can put you on cloud nine or send you to weeping hollow, depending on whether they like or dislike the change.

Can you believe that! The influence we have on other people is tremendous. We can impart glee or grief to others, depending on our words or actions. We can "make their day" or we can rain on their parade. Now, down through the years, I have also watched to see those people who deliver the influence of sunlight.

While I was serving Bluff Springs Baptist Church near Magnolia, Mississippi, we had a deacon named Louie Smith. Louie was as common as an old shoe. He did not have much education and was not well read except for his Bible. However, Louie did, during my time as pastor, always spread sunshine on my life. It made no difference whether he was cleaning the churchyard, visiting the hospital, or leading the singing, he would smile and do his best. Louie made me a better man when he was around. I felt better knowing he was present and will always be thankful for him. He was not the only one, for there have been many others who have made me a better person. Do you know of such people in your own life? Now, that is the kind of person I want to be. I want folks to say when I am dead and gone that life is sweeter because I came along. I want to be wings of joy and not weeping willows.

Jesus talked to His followers on the mountain and said, "Ye are the salt of the earth." You see, salt does a lot but one thing it does is make us thirsty. Jesus said, in effect, "You are to make people thirsty." Yes, as we pass through life let us not be like two ships at sea just trying to not collide, but let us brush up against one another and make each other thirsty. Let our presence, whether by word or action, cause folks to want to know more about God. Thank You, Jesus, for all the Louie Smiths You have caused to rub shoulders with me. Now, even as I say thanks, help me to remember that after "thanks" there is always "giving." Help me as I go about my task this day to seek to make others thirsty for Thee. Let others drink from my stream of joy, but let neither of us forget the Spring.

Trivial Pursuit

Matthew 6:33 *"Seek ye first the kingdom of God."*

One of our favorite pasttimes in Petal, Mississippi, was to gather in front of Roy's Cafe. Especially during the summer months, we would sit and talk for hours. Needless to say, we usually talked about things of no earthly value. Most of the news and events we discussed would be found in the modern-day parlor game called Trivial Pursuit. Have you ever thought about how the word *trivial* came about? I am told that some years ago in Rome there was an inn located at the intersection of three roads. It was here that soldiers would gather to drink and discuss meaningless news and events. *Tri* is the word meaning three and *via*, means way, thus, three ways, The Trivia Inn. Through the years these discussions became known as trivial. Now, trivial, according to the dictionary, means of little value, unimportant, or insignificant.

The modern game of Trivial Pursuit is certainly a commentary on our times. Christians today are busy playing trivial pursuit. I am not speaking of the parlor game, but of playing with their life. We have spent the best part of our life like guys on the street corner or the soldiers in the inn. In every town you can always find a park, a downtown bench, or some other spot where many of the old men of the city will sit for hours, investing their precious time in trivial matters.

It has been my experience over the years that most people in the churches I have pastored are not bad people. When I say that, I am thinking in terms of the fact that if you asked them if they wanted to do wrong, they would say no. Were you to ask them if they wanted to do right, they would say yes. They had no real intention of going against God. They really wanted to be better Christians. Indeed, they were not bad people. Their problem was that they just had God too far down the list. They wanted to live better, but the things like studying the Bible, praying, and witnessing were so far down on their priority list that they never had time to do them. They had invested their lives in the trivial matters. There is a place for community work, sports, recreation, relaxation, and all the other matters that are connected to this passing life, but they should be far down the list.

Jesus gave us the order of the day when He said, "Seek ye first the kingdom of God, and his righteousness; and all these things shall be added unto you." Of course, He spoke this in the midst of a discussion of anxiety over what his followers were to eat and wear. Now, none of us wants our family to go without food or clothing, but neither do we want them to suffer spiritual deficits. You can give yourself for the "other things" and miss the spiritual or you can give yourself to the spiritual first and God will add all the other things necessary for your life.

This is a good day for each of us to take stock and see just how much of our day's activities are spent in trivial pursuits. How much time do we give each week to the small, meaningless, unimportant, insignificant, and things of little value? Most of us will be amazed because we will find the reason we do not have time to allow God to use us more is that we are too busy investing in trivial pursuits.

Hurry Up and Wait

Hebrews 12:1   *"Let us run with patience the race that is set before us."*

We were all standing in one room when a man in a military uniform came in. He stood for a moment looking us over and then said, "OK, you have your choice. You can enlist for three years or thirty-six months. Now, what will it be?" Naturally, I took the three years. I mean, who would want to be away from home for thirty-six months? The next thing I knew folks in other countries were singing my dentist's favorite song, "The Yanks Are Coming." Now, the military was really not that bad. A friend of mine had read the slogan *Join the Navy and See the World.* He joined all right, but they did not tell him he would see it through a porthole. Man, I joined the Army to see the world and felt like I walked around it before I got out of boot camp. You know, in the Army you walk everywhere you go.

A friend of mine said when he enlisted they promised them a free ride. The sergeant said they would ride to boot camp, ride to the training fields, and, if they joined the paratroopers, they would ride them to the jump field and then have a truck pick them up after the jump. It would then ride them back to the camp. He said two men jumped one day and their parachute did not open. One man turned to the other and said, "That lying sergeant, this chute did not open." The other man, whose chute also failed to open, said, "Yeah, and I bet those trucks will not be there when we land either."

While I was stationed in Korea with the U. S. Army, one morning we were placed on red alert. We packed all of our equipment and moved into the field. We were positioned very near the demilitarized zone. This is the border dividing North and South Korea. Everyone knew something was up, but no one was talking. Several days later, we learned we were there in response to President Kennedy's quarantine of Cuba. This was a military move to prevent North Korea from striking back by invading South Korea. The only problem was they did not give us live ammunition. Of course, we could have stood on the hill like we did when we were children and shouted, "Bang, bang, you are dead." Thank the Lord nothing happened. After about a week, we returned to camp.

My problem with the Army was, "Hurry up and wait." They always wanted you to be in a hurry to get where you were going and then when you got there, you had to wait. Everywhere we went there was a line. With my luck, I would go somewhere and there would be no line; then someone would draw one. You know, the military life is sort of like the Christian experience. It is hurry up and wait. Evangelism is certainly urgent. We need to be in a hurry to be saved and to help others find the Lord, but once you are inside the kingdom it is "wait." You cannot mature fast. You cannot become a full-grown saint overnight. Sometimes we expect folks who have been saved a very short time to act like others who have been Christians for years.

We often want the Lord to act fast for us. We pray for patience: "Lord, I need patience and I need it right now." I am thankful for the military and what it taught me. I have learned to be patient with myself and with others. I was just thinking it would be great if we could all be as patient with God, ourselves, our family, and others. I mean, if we could be just as patient with them as we are waiting on the fish to bite!

My Friend Downey

1 Corinthians 15:22 *"Even so in Christ shall all be made alive."*

Today is Good Friday. Sunday morning I will be preaching on the subject of the resurrection of Jesus. I have just hung up the phone. Turning to look at the message I have been working on, I thought how fitting that I should have been working on a message about the resurrection of Jesus when word came that my friend, Reverend P. E. Downey, had just gone to be with the Lord. The news came while I was at home and I had returned to the office to call Mrs. Downey. During our conversation she said he was lying on the couch where he spent most of his time these days. Lois, his daughter, had spent most of the day with him. Downey had been sick for the past several years, but these final days had been worse. Mrs. Downey said that he did not suffer. He just took a long breath and closed his eyes and slipped out to go be with Jesus.

After talking with her on the phone, I thought it best to write my feelings down. First, there is a sadness because Downey had always been a pillar for me. Every time as a young preacher I needed advice or help I turned to him. Although in the past few years we had been miles apart, I still knew he was there. Secondly, I know now how Timothy felt when he lost that great man of God named Paul. Downey had been my Paul. He took me in as a young preacher and taught me how to visit. He showed me how to win people to the Lord. He made me memorize the Bible. I shall always be in debt to him. Thirdly, he taught me to love people. He never refused to help folks. Our ministry together for the most part was spent in the poor sections of Petal and Hattiesburg. Downey used to say, "God loves everybody and we must tell everybody." So he went about his full-time job in public work and pastored what was then Petal Harvey Mission. A full-time church now stands in another part of Petal because this man and his family were faithful to the Lord.

My feelings are mixed. I am sad for Bruce, Lois, and Mrs. Downey and the grandchildren. I know all of them will miss him greatly. I feel alone, yet I know I am not. My heart tells me there is so much I should have said to him, but now he is gone. My head tells me he is better off with Jesus, but there is still an empty place in my heart. There is a hurt because I know I should be there with the family, but I have responsibilities here. There is no way I can be in my church this Easter and also be with his family for the funeral. I guess the best thing would be to have a talk with Downey. That is it! I'll pretend!

"Come on in, Jerry. Sit there on the sofa," Downey spoke as he took a seat in his favorite chair. "Listen, Downey, I have a problem," I said. "Good," said he and crossed his legs straight out in front of him. "Hey, I guess you know you are not here any more," and as I spoke, I could tell he had a smile on his face. "Well, Son, it was time to go," he said. "The Lord has appointed a time for all of us and I was ready." "Yes, I know, but you have me in a fix. You see, I have to decide whether it is more important to preach on Sunday or go to your funeral." He smiled and his eyes lit up. "You remember what I told you years ago?" "Yes, you said that when you have an opportunity to preach, preach, and those I believe were your very words." Then in my mind I thought, *But what about the family?* Downey knew what I was thinking. He leaned forward in his chair. "If you are worried about Mrs. Downey, Lois, and the rest, don't," he said. "You know they are burying me on Easter and they bury me with the hope of seeing me again. We are all on a journey and I am just going on ahead so I can make a few arrangements before they get there." With that remark he leaned back in his chair. "OK, then, it is settled; I will preach this Sunday." I looked down at the floor and waited for him to respond. There was no answer and when I looked up my friend was gone.

Easter came and I preached in my church. The family gathered and placed Downey in the grave in Petal, Mississippi. Easter will always be special to me. That is the day my Lord arose from the dead and that is the day they buried my friend, Downey, my apostle Paul, with the hope that he will one day rise, too.

Fun Being His

Philippians 1:21   *"For to me to live is Christ."*

While speaking to a group of preachers in Florida, Jess Moody gave three points that I have never forgotten. Jess said, "It is not fun not being His." He went on to explain how sad a life is without Jesus. Secondly, he said, "It is fun being His." In this part of the sermon he spoke of the joy of being a Christian. Thirdly, he said, "I have also learned it is not fun being His but not all His." Now, this was where the sermon began to rub. We all knew we were His (God's), but we also knew we were not all His. You see, the lordship of Christ is not a once-for-all decision. Yes, we decide to give our life to Him, but to bring our life under His lordship daily is a moment-by-moment decision.

Is not this where we all live? We start the day being His because we belong to Him. Then somewhere along the way we act independently of Him and all of a sudden we find it is not fun being His when we are not all His. The joy of His fellowship is broken. Oh, we have not lost our sonship, but we have caused a break in the fellowship with our Father.

The lordship of Jesus begins with a decision but continues as a daily exercise. That exercise of our faith is what we call discipleship. Then as we are being discipled we will see the reign of God in our life. Of course, as God reigns in our life the end result of His reign is His release through our life. Paul states it this way in Philippians 1:21, "To me to live is Christ." When moment by moment my goal is to allow Jesus to live His life through me, then the result of His release is the reward of seeing God in my life. Some of that reward is to know it is fun being His, especially when you are all His.

Part of the problem is that most of us see sin as an act. Indeed, if we can just control the act, then we have taken care of the problem. The fact is that when you shut off one act, then sin manifests itself in some other act. Sin is a condition before God. Any time we act independently of God we have sinned. The Book of Romans says, "Whatsoever is not of faith is sin" (14:23).

Some time ago I read of a lady who was killed in an automobile accident. She was eating a sandwich when the head-on collision occurred. The fact is that while preparing to live, she died. In the Christian faith we live by preparing to die. Truly it is the death, the submission of our will to His will moment by moment that helps us understand it is fun being His, especially when we are all His.

How do we die daily or moment by moment to self and live for God? Let me suggest that it is like you are sitting at the table with your wife. She says, "Did you know Charlie and Mary are leaving town?" You hardly look up from the morning paper as she pleads, "Did you hear me?" Well, of course, you heard her; or did you? You see, to really hear means we have an appropriate response. Really she was asking you to give her your undivided attention. You heard her with your ears, but you did not pay much attention.

God must have this problem with us! We hear Him, but we do not give Him our undivided attention. We may even deny ourself things, but the Bible speaks of "denying self." Some call this crucifying self, but that is impossible. If you get one hand and both feet nailed to the cross, how are you going to nail the other hand? You cannot crucify self. Ah, but Paul gives us the answer. "I am crucified with Christ." I do not have to die; I am already dead. You say that is true, but I also am alive. You are right. But being alive is Christ living in me "and the life which I now live in the flesh I live by the faith of the Son of God" (Gal. 2:20).

You may say it all sounds tricky, but it is as simple as the nose on your face. The secret is moment by moment giving your life to Jesus, and you too will find it is fun being His, especially when you are all His.

Mule Eggs for Sale

Matthew 13:22

"He also that received seed among the thorns is he that heareth the word; and the care of this world, and the deceitfulness of riches, choke the word, and he becometh unfruitful."

Robert Knippers of Magnolia, Mississippi, has had a lot of strange stories told on him, but perhaps this is one of the best. It seems that Mr. Knippers had several mules that he wanted to sell. He ran a brief ad in the local *Magnolia Gazette* and before you know it folks came from every nook and cranny. Robert sold all of the mules he had for one hundred dollars each. Several days later two boys from Louisiana pulled up into his yard in an old beat-up Ford pickup truck. They jumped out and ran toward the porch. Robert had been out in the yard feeding the chickens, so he still had on his barnyard clothes. As he came through the dog yard, the two young men from Louisiana were leaning on the fence. Robert had heard them drive up, so he asked, "What can I do for you fellows?" They looked at each other and smiled. Then the big tall one said, "We want to buy one of those mules you had advertised in the paper."

Robert dropped his feed bucket and gave them the sad news that he had no more mules to sell. Well, those two old boys were so brokenhearted they almost started to cry. Then Robert said, "Wait, fellows!" and he disappeared around the side of the house. While in the backyard, Robert took two watermelons and sprayed them white. The paint was hardly dry when he walked around the house with a watermelon under each arm saying, "Fellows, I am sold out of mules, but you can have these two mule eggs for the price of one mule." Needless to say, they bought the two mule eggs and headed back to Louisiana.

About ten miles into Louisiana, they hit a large hole in the road. The mule eggs (watermelons) popped out of the back of the truck and burst as they hit the road. Now, right where they hit was a big Louisiana jackrabbit. This frightened the rabbit and he took off across the highway in front of the pickup. Those two boys from Louisiana gave chase. About an hour later one of the boys stopped and said, "Herbert, let that baby mule go, we cannot plow anything that runs that fast anyway."

Christians are too smart to buy mule eggs, but many times we are deceived. If we are deceived it means we have been cheated or fallen prey to a false impression either by appearance, statement, or influence. The Bible says that sometimes we are deceived by riches. Jesus said, "He also that received seed among the thorns is he that heareth the word; and the care of this world, and the deceitfulness of riches, choke the word, and he becometh unfruitful" (Matt. 13:22). Hebrews 3:13 says it this way: "Exhort one another daily, while it is called To-day; lest any of you be hardened through the deceitfulness of sin."

Sin is the devil's mule egg. He will always deceive us. Christians can never use deceit. This is a tool of the devil. In Colossians Paul called it "vain." He says, "Beware lest any man spoil you through philosophy and vain deceit" (2:8). Deceit is empty whether by word or deed; it is void of anything profitable. We must not be deceived by the devil or someone else; we must not try to deceive others; we must be careful not to deceive ourselves. Hear the writer of Galatians say, "If a man think himself to be something, when he is nothing, he deceiveth himself" (6:3). You see, even self-conceit is self-deceit. When one is conceited he has bought the devil's mule egg. First Thessalonians 2:3 says, "For our exhortation was not of deceit."

If we, as children of God, stray out of God's will, if we are off the beaten path, if we are not following His will for our life, we have, in fact, bought the devil's mule egg. And soon, like the two boys from Louisiana, we, too, will find "we cannot plow anything that runs that fast."

Staying on Track

Proverbs 3:6 *"In all thy ways acknowledge him, and he shall direct thy paths."*

Terry moved about the radio station with the greatest of ease. My sister-in-law, Linday Bartly, was working for him as his secretary and bookkeeper. We talked for a few minutes and he explained how he was able to be the disc jockey and work the total program of the station. Now, for most of us, this would not be much of a problem, but it was for Terry. You see, he is blind.

Almost a year later I was watching channel 3's (WLBT-Jackson, MS) ten o'clock news when the Spirit of Mississippi Award came on. This station had been honoring men and women across our state who had helped our state become a better place to live. On this night I was especially interested because I knew the young man they were interviewing. It was strange that the man conducting the interview was the same man who had turned Terry down for a job several years before while he was working as a disc jockey at a radio station. He had, in fact, told Terry that day that he should seek some other kind of employment. It was interesting to see the same man who now was employed by this television station interview Terry,

Staying on Track

who now owned his own radio station (WTWZ, Clinton, MS) and was the only disc jockey.

During the interview, Terry was asked something to the effect, "How did you achieve this dream?" I shall never forget his answer. He gave us a clue to how any of us can achieve goals we set in life. Terry replied, "I did one thing every day toward my goal. No matter how small I found something I could do every day that would help me reach my goal."

Winners always make commitments while a loser makes excuses or promises. An achiever says, "I may not be as good as others, but I am working at it." A loser will say, "I am not as bad as some people I know." A successful person looks for a better way to do it but a loser says, "This is the way we have always done it." John D. Rockefeller, Jr., said, "The secret of success is to do the common things uncommonly well." You can bet the road to success will be a provider of many tempting parking places. Everybody has a sad story to tell but the world wants to see the baby, not hear about the labor pains. So what am I saying? It really is very simple. A lot of people have advice about success, but I think Terry said it best. He said, "We must do something every day that keeps us in line and on line to achieve our goal." This is true in sports. It is true in business. As a matter of fact, I cannot think of any area that it is not true.

If staying on target is true in other fields, it is equally true in the area of our faith. Samson missed success because he let Delilah get him off course. David missed the fullness God had for him because of Bathsheba. Moses let his temper get him off base and he was called out when it came to going into the Promised Land. Lot "pitched his tent toward Sodom." Solomon strayed from the right path when he "loved many strange women." Esau took a wrong turn when he sold his birthright for a bowl of soup. Cain traveled a crooked road when he killed his brother Abel. Jonah moved out on a side street when he became angry because the people of Nineveh repented and God did not destroy them. John Mark left the main road when he walked away from the missionary journey with Paul. Let each of us today do at least one thing to keep us on track toward our goal of becoming like Jesus. Could this be what Paul meant when he said, "This one thing I do . . ." (Phil. 3:13)?

You Can Go Home Again

Luke 15:18   *"I will arise and go to my father."*

    Several days ago a young couple in our church related the story of their young daughter's first night away from home. A friend had talked her into spending the night with her. Everything was all right as long as they were busy and having fun. However, when the night grew late and time came to go to bed the little girl began sobbing. She cried so hard that her parents finally had to come in the middle of the night and take her home. Once in the father's arms the little girl said, "I wanted to come home, Daddy."

    Oh! Here is a confession that has sobbed its way through the centuries. It is the cry of the prodigal. A young man was away from home and he was having fun. Once the fun was over, sitting on the pig fence of life he cried, "I want to go home." This is the confession of one of the best-known personalities of the New Testament. It speaks to those who climb some hill of difficulty, perhaps in the valley of defeat. It speaks to those down and out, saying this can happen to you. You can go home again.

    I have asked myself a hundred times, how did the

young man get into the far country? Did he just wake up one morning and decide that he would ruin his life? No! We do not start the day with the idea of having some tragedy befall us. This young man was as normal as you and I. He wanted life and he wanted to live it on the edge. He wanted to be happy! So he turned being sick of home into homesickness. He exchanged his father's home for a pigpen. He changed his dream into failure. Why and how? He wanted to be free, but more important than that he wanted only to please himself. He set out on a life that would answer only to himself. He was his own man. He would do as he pleased whether it pleased anyone else or not.

Let us remember that it is the spring of selfishness from which all the streams of sin will flow. Selfishness is expensive. Ask Adam and Eve in the land near the Garden of Eden. Ask Samson as he pulls the pillars of that giantic building down. Ask David as he looks at the long finger of Nathan, the prophet. You see, this young man wanted to be free, but selfishness is never freedom. In the end he was sent to the pigpen. He did not choose to go; he was sent. He lost his freedom because he sought to keep it.

I have heard the masters play the piano and they were super. However, when I sit down at the piano I want freedom. I do not follow any music. Notes are not for me. Why, I just play what I want when I want and no one wants to hear me play. You see, I am free, but I am a prisoner of my own freedom. I cannot express myself through music because I do not follow the rules of music. When you and I seek to hold on to our life we are selfish and we lose it. If we turn loose and give our life to God then we truly find ourselves and we are free.

You know, the real tragedy of the prodigal is that he was where he was needlessly. He made some bad choices that led him to the pigpen. Had he been put there I would feel sorry for him. Had hard times struck I could give him a little room, but he was there by choice. I am just glad the story does not end there. He got up and went home to the arms of a waiting, forgiving father. Perhaps you want to recall now those happy moments in your life when you went home to the Father. Maybe some readers will find time now to move away from that selfish life and learn that they too can still go home to the Father.

Look for Me When You See Me Coming

Matthew 24:36 *"But of that day and hour knoweth no man, no, not the angels of heaven, but my Father only."*

My father used to drive us nuts. When he left the house he would never tell us what time to expect him back home. Now, you say, he should have and we would have all agreed, but not Dad. His words still ring true today as they did then. I can still see him walking down the steps of the front porch and I can hear Mom say, "Earl, what time do you think you will be back?" He stopped, turned, and looked back at all of us. "Look for me when you see me coming." Then he would walk away. There were two things this did for us. First of all, we expected him to return home at any moment. Secondly, we were constantly looking for him. Every time a car came down the old dirt road we fought the dust and ran to the front to meet him. Sure, we were disappointed many times when it was not Dad, but each disappointment seemed to heighten the excitement for his return.

Have you found that some Christians are all caught up in the second coming of Jesus? Some have maps, signs, and symbols. Many have it all figured out. Now that is fine with me. However, I must admit sometimes I just can't buy all they have to say. Oh, I know He is coming. No doubt about that. There are two things I am certain about. I will die and be with Him when He comes, or I will still be alive and leave with Him when He comes. So either way, my future is all wrapped up in Jesus and that is what counts.

We need to be careful about dates and times. A careful reading of the New Testament will let us know that even the angels in heaven are not given a hint about the return of Jesus. Some in Paul's day got so carried away with the second coming that they just sat down and would not work. Paul had the answer for that. He said, "If any would not work, neither should he eat" (2 Thess. 3:10). Someone said we do not need to be occupied with His coming, but we need to be occupied until He does come. This is where I think we need to place our emphasis.

When Jesus told the parable about the nobleman who left ten servants in charge of his wealth, he emphasized they were to "Occupy till I come" (Luke 19:13). We need to be working. Then, on the other hand, we need to be watching. I was told of a small school in which retarded children were not only taught the ABC's, but also the Bible. The teacher is reported to have said that it was impossible to keep the windows in the building clean. When once the children heard the story of the second coming of Jesus, she said at every break they would run to the window. There they pressed their dirty little fingers and faces hard against the window straining, watching, looking, to see if Jesus was coming.

Certainly that is one way to watch. However, as children we watched for Dad even when we were not looking. You see, we were expecting him any minute. Since he could come any minute we were always ready to drop everything and run to meet him. We also made sure we were not doing anything that he would not want us to be doing when he came. We were like the five wise virgins in Matthew who took their lamps and went forth to meet the bridegroom. The early church believed Jesus would return in their lifetime, and it certainly made a difference in how they lived.

The problem many church members face today is that they have so many signs to be fulfilled that Jesus can't come back for another hundred years or so. Now, if we knew Dad would not be back until Saturday we also knew we had several days when we could get away with a lot. We could let some chores go undone and do them just before he came home. Now I know my Dad never studied psychology, but he knew how to keep us wondering, working, and watching.

Just the other day I walked out of the house and my son said, "When will you be back?" I turned and replied, "Look for me when you see me coming!"

Keepers of the Well

Song of Solomon 1:6 *"But mine own vineyard have I not kept."*

The community of Lakeview was a small rural setting that almost any Southern boy would have been proud to grow up in. We had the Hattiesburg Brick Yard which provided us with many playful hours. There were several lakes from which the name Lakeview was derived. Around those lakes a park had existed during World War II. The park had in the past boomed on Sunday afternoons with soldiers from Camp Shelby. There was in our community the Top and Bottom Water Works. This was the main water supply for the city of Hattiesburg. In between the waterworks were plenty of hills and woods to amuse any boy. We also had our own railroad tracks, Mixon Creek, Bouie River, and the Mississippi Power Company substation. Needless to say, a boy could find lots of things to do in our community of Lakeview.

There was just north of our house back near the river a spring. This artesian water flowed freely and I can remember many happy hours spent drinking from its clear, cool fountain. It made no difference whether we came early in the morning and started the day with a drink or if we came at high noon, the water always flowed freely, tingling your tongue because it was so cold.

That was some time ago. As a matter of years it was almost forty years ago. On this day as I paused to drink from its cool flow once again, I was somewhat shocked. There was a terrible smell in the air. As I walked from my automobile it was difficult to remember where the spring was located, but I was sure I was going in the right direction.

As I brushed the limbs back I realized I had once again found the spring of my youth. It was then I discovered where the smell was coming from. There was no sound from its ice water bubbling up from the ground. Instead, it was filled with limbs, slime, and green moss. There was hardly a sound. The slime and debris had filled the old spring, choking off its free-flowing waters. Now there seemed to be only death. What had happened? As I think back over my youth, I can remember each time we drank from the spring we would always pick up any limb or trash that had fallen near or in the spring. We had been the keepers of the well. Now the keepers of the well had departed and the result was that a bubbling spring had become only a trickle flowing into a swamp filled with disease and death.

Is this not what happens in our Christian experience? We are the keepers of the well. Many of us will have to say with Solomon, "mine own vineyard have I not kept" (Song of Sol. 1:6). When Jesus spoke of a river flowing out of the believer in John 7:38, He had in mind not so much that the flow was from God, but that it was God that flowed. God was actually flowing through their lives to others. Of course, as He flowed He gave strength for life to the believer and to others.

Today, we need to see if God is actually flowing through

our life. Are we channels of blessings to others or have we become stagnant? Perhaps our springs have been filled with debris from the world. Could it be that the flow of the Spirit has been stifled by our hatred, laziness, indifference, and envy? Or maybe the limbs of lust or the jagged bark of jealousy have clogged our spring. One truth is ever clearer to me now after my return to the spring. If the spring is to flow freely with clear cool, refreshing water, someone will have to be the keeper of the well. When the well is clean, the water is clear.

Clear water is always a call to others to "Come. And let him who is athirst come. And whosoever will, let him take the water of life freely" (Rev. 22:17). We are the keepers of the well.

Home Before Dark

2 Samuel 22:29 "*The Lord will lighten my darkness.*"

Luke 15:20 "*But when he was yet a great way off, his father saw him.*"

My bare feet left footprints in the front yard. There was no grass because Mom saw that we kept it swept with sagebrush brooms made from a field near the house. I pulled my short-legged pants up higher on my hips and turned to wave good-bye. "We will be up behind the brickyard playing this afternoon." Mom smiled and walked back toward the front door. As I turned to walk up the gravel drive she shouted. "Be home before dark."

There is something about the dark that we all dread. I remember as a child we never liked to sleep in a room that was dark. The Mixon graveyard just down from our house was a place of darkness. Why, we did not like to even go in the church house when it was dark. Perhaps you can remember those nights when you or your child lay sick and you wished for the day. There is just something about the darkness that we do not like.

Throughout the Bible we come to understand that darkness is always seen as something evil. God and His goodness are always seen as light. There is even in the heart of each believer a sense of fear as he faces death.

Yes, we have faith but there is that certain uncertainty that we dread. Death in some of the old hymns was expressed by darkness as we come to the river Jordan.

I shall never forget that afternoon we spent playing on the red clay hills behind the brickyard. Memory fails me about what all we did and even those who were my playmates, but I do remember the lingering shadows. When once we discovered darkness creeping in, we all ran as fast as we could trying to outrace the giant shadows. I remember that in the darkness I froze as in the distance a large bear stood in the path. Friendly trees now appeared to be wild animals or, worse, some devil leaping out at us. Once I remember being caught on a bush but for fear it was a demon I pulled so hard my pants came off and I ran the final distance home in my underwear.

A sigh of relief always came as we dashed through the yard and at last reached the front porch. As Mom opened the screen door and the light darted into the yard, it was then we realized angry demons were nothing more than friendly trees or familiar objects. Standing on the porch and looking back toward the brickyard the distant hill was silhouetted against the evening sky. There from my father's house all the pain and fear of the journey home now seemed to vanish. I could see it all now. There was no real need to fear.

When once we were sent off to bed, I can remember many a time that Mom would say, "Jerry, I told you to be home before dark." Then, as I gave my many excuses and told of the weird and strange creatures that attacked, I was comforted by the memory of her standing on the porch. As she folded the blanket back and walked from the room, she would say, "There was no need to be afraid; I was watching for you from the porch."

My dear saint, the shadows may be drawing about life.

You may have strayed from the Father's love, or perhaps failure to live for God has caused your life to drift into the darkness. Familiar friends and things appear evil and shapeless demons may taunt your soul. Take heart; God is watching from the front porch and you, too, will be home before dark.